WINNING LIKE SACHIN

In a career spanning nineteen years, **Devendra Prabhudesai** has worked across sectors and handled a wide range of responsibilities—from working with the police to rehabilitate victims of crime, to executing some of the biggest cricketing events organized in India in recent times. An author, screenwriter and anchor, he was also the Manager for Media Relations & Corporate Affairs at the Board of Control for Cricket in India (BCCI) from January 2008 to July 2015.

Devendra lives in Mumbai with his wife, Anuradha, and children, Abhimanyu and Ira.

Also by the same author

A Biography of Rahul Dravid:
The Nice Guy Who Finished First (2005)

SMG: A Biography of Sunil Manohar Gavaskar (2009)

Hero: A Biography of Sachin Ramesh Tendulkar (2017)

WINNING LIKE SACHIN

THINK & SUCCEED LIKE TENDULKAR

DEVENDRA PRABHUDESAI

RUPA

Published by
Rupa Publications India Pvt. Ltd 2018
7/16, Ansari Road, Daryaganj
New Delhi 110002

Sales centres:
Allahabad Bengaluru Chennai
Hyderabad Jaipur Kathmandu
Kolkata Mumbai

ISBN: 978-81-291-5175-9

Third impression 2018

10 9 8 7 6 5 4 3

Printed at Saurabh Printers Private Limited, Greater Noida.

To

Amitabh Bachchan & Sunil Gavaskar,

my childhood heroes

Contents

Introduction

'A hero is someone who has given his or her life to something bigger than oneself.'

—Joseph Campbell

Sachin Ramesh Tendulkar captured the imagination of the nation as a teenager in the winter of 1989. That he would play for India was never doubted by those who had followed his cricketing exploits on the maidans (grounds) of Mumbai, his hometown, since the mid-1980s. However, not many expected him to represent the country at the young age of sixteen.

The youngest member of the Indian team that toured Pakistan in November 1989 was by no means raw and untested. He was Mumbai's highest scorer in the 1988–89 season of the Ranji Trophy with an aggregate of 349 runs, his best performance being a century in his debut game. He had already visited England twice, in 1988 and 1989 respectively, with boys of his age group on 'educational' cricketing tours, and of course, he had played and plundered bowling attacks in junior-level tournaments—from inter-school to inter-zonal—since 1984–85.

The first Test match of Sachin Tendulkar's career began at Karachi's National Stadium on 15 November 1989. His 200th and last Test ended exactly twenty-four years and one day later, across the Arabian Sea, at Mumbai's Wankhede Stadium, on 16 November 2013. He accomplished a fair bit in between.

The teenage prodigy went on to become an icon for generations. Most of the batting records in the history of the sport, in Tests and One-Day Internationals (ODIs), presently stand in his name. He was the most influential member of a cricket team that did India proud.

> A nation that had long been used to lagging behind, whether in economics or sports, now boasted the world's best batsman and went on to become world champions again, 28 years after our first triumph. The No.1 ranking in both Tests and ODIs is no longer an impossible dream: we have held both, at different times. Television revenues from the growing and increasingly prosperous Indian audience have transformed India's place in world cricket too: today some 80 per cent of the global game's resources are generated by India. As a result, in the cheerful words of a senior BCCI official, India is to the ICC what the USA is to the UN Security Council, the one country that all other

> members find indispensable—and impossible to ignore. Tendulkar's 24 years in top-flight cricket eerily mirror the transformation of India at the cusp of the 21st century. There is an Indian Dream, and in his own lifetime, Tendulkar is its Prophet.
>
> —Shashi Tharoor,
> 'The Sachin Sunset', *Wisden India*, November 2013

Sachin Tendulkar achieved a lot more than just victories and distinctions. For nearly a quarter of a century, he personified excellence. A quick learner, he proved that talent was nothing unless it was complemented with tenacity. He showed that the world could be conquered by combining honesty and humility. He abhorred living in the past and resting on his laurels. He spared no effort to enhance his skills and proficiency. Whenever confronted by a crisis or criticism, he never cribbed. Instead, he returned to the drawing board, introspected and then responded to his critics with his deeds on the cricket field—never with words. While he was always mindful of his position in the team's hierarchy, regardless of whether he was the 'official' captain or not, he never abused it. For him, a leader's duties and responsibilities were paramount. The rights and privileges that he enjoyed as a leader came a distant second.

Unlike a former Pakistani cricketing legend, who declared himself a 'Triple PhD' in cricket, men like Sachin and Sir Donald Bradman—widely regarded as the greatest batsmen the game has ever seen—always considered themselves students of the sport. At no point in their careers did they see themselves as bigger than the game. Their chosen profession reciprocated their love and respect for it.

Sachin supplemented his passion for his profession with three more Ps—patience, penance and perseverance. He possessed the six Cs—Clarity of thought, the ability to display Courage and Character in a crisis, a flair to Communicate and Collaborate effectively, and, of course, Commitment.

> 'Pursue excellence, not success. If you achieve excellence, then success will have no option but to pursue you.'
>
> —*3 Idiots* (2009)

His commitment to excellence yielded success, and with it came the rewards. Sachin became the highest-earning Indian sportsperson in 1995 when he was signed by the US-based WorldTel for an incredible US$7.5 million (₹31.5 crore), for a period of five years. The contract with WorldTel was renewed in 2001 with a price tag of ₹100 crore. Five years later, he signed a three-year deal worth ₹180 crore with Iconix. *Forbes* magazine estimated that he was the highest-earning Indian cricketer before being eclipsed by Mahendra Singh Dhoni in 2010. In his prime, Sachin endorsed nearly twenty prominent brands.

Four years into his retirement, the maestro is making waves as an ace entrepreneur. Sachin co-owns the Kerala Blasters, a team in the Indian Super (Football) League. He also co-owns Tamil Thalaivas, a team that participates in the Pro-Kabaddi League and the Bengaluru Blasters outfit that plays in the Premier Badminton League. He has done some remarkable work as a Member of Parliament and contributed actively to the well-being of society by being the United Nations International Children's Fund's (UNICEF) Ambassador for hygiene and sanitation. He also represents the Swachh Bharat (Clean India) campaign.

In the pages to follow, I have endeavoured to showcase and illustrate the various attributes that make the youngest recipient of the Bharat Ratna—the country's highest civilian honour—the ideal role model, not only for aspiring cricketers, but also professionals wishing to make a mark in the greatest sport of all—life.

I hope the readers find this book as interesting and inspirational as the individual it seeks to spotlight.

Devendra Prabhudesai
26 February 2018

1

No Shortcut to Success

Start Early, Work Hard, Stay Focused

It was Ajit Tendulkar, Sachin's brother, who took the initiative to 'structure' his younger sibling's life. This was in 1984, when the pre-teen, the youngest member of a family that comprised his parents, two elder brothers and an elder sister, was keeping himself occupied by indulging in a series of pranks with his friends in Sahitya Sahawas, the housing complex where they lived. Ajit, a talented cricketer who had represented his school and college with a reasonable amount of success, had observed his younger sibling's aptitude for the sport while watching him in action on the playground of the complex. He reckoned that Sachin had potential that could be tapped and the only individual who could do so optimally was Ramakant Achrekar, who conducted nets at Shivaji Park, the nursery of Mumbai cricket. Ajit met the coach at the start of Sachin's summer holidays in 1984.

Achrekar's first impression of the eleven-year-old in the nets was not positive. He suggested to Ajit that he bring his kid brother back when he was older. However, Ajit pleaded and reasoned, and finally won the day. Sachin was inducted in the nets and into competitive cricket.

In the days to follow, the boy took to the nets like a duck to water. Achrekar noticed that his new pupil tended to grip the handle of the bat very low, close to its shoulder. This was because Sachin was using Ajit's bat, which was on the taller and heavier side for him. He held it closer to its shoulder to be able to control it better.

Achrekar tried to get Sachin to grip the handle in the middle, as was dictated by the coaching manual. However, the pupil's hands would slip down after some time. The coach finally relented when he realized that Sachin was batting well despite his 'unorthodox' grip.

As the days passed, the coach's fondness for his ward grew. Achrekar asked Sachin what he did after the practice session concluded at 10.00 a.m. Sachin replied that he spent the afternoons with his friends at Sahitya Sahawas. Achrekar promptly instructed him to report back for nets in the afternoons as well. The boy was taken aback by the diktat. He was slightly peeved to miss out on the opportunity to fool around with his childhood buddies. However, he was overruled by the cricketer within him. The sudden transformation of the happy-go-lucky youngster into a driven sportsperson surprised everybody who had known him as a child, his friends included.

A few weeks later, it was his family's turn to be surprised. Achrekar contacted Professor Ramesh Tendulkar, Sachin's father, and apprised him about his son's cricketing talent. Sachin's father was a creative and versatile individual who taught Marathi language and literature and wrote poetry. The coach was of the view that Sachin had it in him to go a long way in the sport. It was therefore prudent that he be given access to the ladder of competitive cricket. The issue was that Bandra IES, the English-medium school where Sachin studied, did not have a cricket team. Achrekar recommended that Sachin shift to Shardashram Vidyamandir, whose English- and Marathi-medium cricket teams were coached by him.

Sahitya Sahawas in Bandra was a fair distance away from Shardashram in Dadar. There was no bus that plied between the two locations directly, which meant that Sachin would have to change buses on the way, that too early in the morning, as the school opened at 7.00 a.m. Besides, he was only eleven at the time. Boys were generally inducted into inter-school cricket when they were studying in Class Seven or Eight. Sachin, on the other hand, was to begin Class Six. The commute to and from Shardashram would eat into his leisure and study time.

Professor Tendulkar could have taken the easy way out and 'played safe'. He could very well have told his son to play cricket during the holidays and concentrate on studies for the rest of the year. He could have put his foot down on the idea of changing schools. But he did not. He and the rest of the family left the final decision to Sachin himself. They assured him that they would back him, regardless of the decision he made.

Little did they know that that was the moment when the boy's life changed and when the history of Indian cricket took an unexpected turn. The youngest member of their family, whom they all doted on, informed them that he was ready for the change, and the challenge.

It was on that day in 1984 that the eleven-year-old Sachin Tendulkar first proved that age was just a number. He had found his calling, and had decided to let his love for cricket, which had grown into a passion under the tutelage of Achrekar, override every other aspect of his life.

Sachin was of course fortunate to have the support of his family. Many cricketing careers have been, and continue to be, nipped in the bud because the parents are reluctant to let their child focus on sports instead of academics. Having said that, luck isn't something one can rely on all the time. It needs to be complemented with commitment.

The young Tendulkar was by no means the only individual whose life was irrevocably altered by an incident that occurred during his or her formative years.

'These things have to be earned, you should not ask for them,' Madhav Mantri, who kept wicket for India in four Test matches in the early 1950s, had told his young pre-teen nephew when the boy requested him to 'lend' some of the items that he had 'earned' and collected during his stint with the national team. These comprised autographed stumps, caps and pullovers. Sunil Gavaskar, the nephew in question, took his uncle's reminder that there was no shortcut to the top, very seriously.

Similarly, the turning point of Kapil Dev's career was his protest against the 'inadequate' food being served at a national camp for junior cricketers in the mid-1970s. The teenaged fast bowler told a senior official that he needed more food as he was a fast bowler. The official just laughed in response and told him that there were no fast bowlers in India. The teenager responded to the jibe by initiating a fast-bowling revolution of sorts in the country, in the years to come.

The weeks and months that followed Sachin's shift to Shardashram took a toll on him, physically and mentally, but he did not give in, not even to a bout of jaundice. To reduce his commute, the family suggested that he move in with his paternal uncle and aunt, who lived a stone's throw away from Shivaji Park. Sachin made the move in the summer of 1985, a full year after he had been inducted into Achrekar's nets.

His inter-school debut for Shardashram was eventful, not because he played some crisp strokes in a knock of 24, but because of a lesson on ethics administered to him by his coach. Since local newspapers only reported individual scores of 30 or higher in their coverage of inter-school cricket, the scorer at the game offered to 'transfer' 6 'extras' to Sachin's individual score. The boy succumbed to the prospect of seeing his name in print for the first time. He was ecstatic when he checked out the paper the following morning, but his coach was livid. A chastened Sachin promised him that he would never take a shortcut again.

The Shardashram boys learnt from their coach that trying to take the shortcut to reach the top amounted to taking the shortcut to mediocrity.

So impressive were Sachin's performances in his very first inter-school season in 1984–85 that some people who had watched him went to the extent of predicting that he would play for the country. This was when he was not even twelve years old.

His routine in the summer holidays of 1985 was extraordinarily hectic. He would attend nets from 7.00 a.m. to 9.30 a.m. If there was a match, he would stay back at the ground. On non-match days, he would return home at 10.00 a.m., and report back at the nets at 3.00 p.m. He would practice till the sun went down. On days when there were matches, he would take to the nets after the game ended at 4.30 pm, and bat till sundown.

He would be so exhausted that he would fall asleep at the dining table itself while his aunt served him dinner.

The twelve-year-old played a mind-boggling fifty-five matches in the sixty-day summer holidays of 1985. Shivaji Park apart, Achrekar conducted nets at the Sassanian Cricket Club at the Azad Maidan in south Mumbai. If Sachin were to be dismissed early in a match being played at the Shivaji Park, Achrekar would take him on his two-wheeler to Azad

Maidan and send him in to bat in another game. The guru swore by match-practice, as it was during these contests that youngsters were exposed to different situations and got opportunities to fine-tune their ability to think on their feet.

Even an adult would have found a schedule like this rigorous, and Sachin was only a teenager. Anybody else would have protested and rebelled. The boy was missing out on the little pleasures of life, after all. At that age, everybody wants to hang out with their friends, watch films and do all those things that regular teenagers are known to do. However, cricket, to him, was paramount. He did not mind making sacrifices to excel in the stream that he had chosen for himself.

He did not know it then, but the next three decades of his life were as much about sacrifices as they were about victories, runs and records. Sachin learnt at a very early age that 'impossible was nothing'. He loved his coach's penchant for pushing his pupils and encouraging them to challenge what they believed were their physical and mental limitations.

> Every time I scored runs, my brother and coach never said 'Well played,' and that is why in my farewell speech (on 16 November 2013), I said to my coach that at least now you can take a chance by saying 'Well done' as there are no more matches in my career, but something that I lived for was appreciation from my coach and

> brother, which never came, and that was something that made me give my best all the time.
>
> —Sachin Tendulkar,
> BMW Presents Sachin Tendulkar, March 2015

In his endeavour to ensure that his ward always kept his feet on the ground, the coach had a willing ally in Ajit Tendulkar. The two of them insisted that Sachin focus on the next game and leave the rest of the world to dwell on the previous game. Either way, Sachin would have sleepless nights. If he had not played well in a game, he would sit up the whole night introspecting and thinking about how he could rectify the mistake he had made. And if he had played well, then he would spend the night identifying what he needed to do to be more successful in the next game.

There was no dearth of cricketing talent in Mumbai in the 1980s. But what set Achrekar's pupils apart was their commitment to the sport.

They trained even when the Mumbai monsoon was at its fiercest. Achrekar would conduct the sessions with an umbrella in hand, even as his wards would play and train in the slush. Most of the other school teams played safe, playing and training during the official season, which lasted from October to May, and then taking a four-month break when rains lashed Mumbai. Training through the year enabled the Shardashram players to get used to each other and get to know each other inside out. This in turn facilitated effective communication and teamwork and helped them produce exceptional performances when the season began.

Achrekar would make Sachin bat in four nets, back-to-back, in the latter stages of the session. If Sachin was getting tired after spending hours in the middle, he never showed it. After four sessions, the coach would ask him to bat in a fifth net on a wearing wicket, against the best bowlers. The coach would flag off this final session by placing a one-rupee coin on the middle stump. The bowler, who would get Sachin out, would win the coin. If Sachin remained unbeaten, the coin would be his.

Sachin made a habit of winning those coins. He collected a fair number of them over the years. Even today, he rates those coins as his most precious possessions. They mean more to him than all the awards that were showered on him in later years.

These accounts prove conclusively that talent is nothing unless it is combined with penance and perseverance. Sachin had the talent, but he had to work himself into the ground to equip himself with the temperament to battle the odds, surmount obstacles and emerge victorious. This in turn enabled him to make optimal use of his talent.

LEARNING TIP

Talent alone cannot ensure success.

It needs to be complemented with hard work.

Sachin was once reprimanded by his coach for opting to watch a match featuring his seniors instead of playing in a game that had been specially organized for him. Achrekar impressed upon him in no uncertain terms that he would be better off giving others the opportunity to clap for him rather than him clapping for others.

While his coach and elder brother guided him on the field, Sachin's father and the rest of the family did their bit off it.

> The one person who has influenced my life the most was my father—Ramesh Tendulkar. My 'baba' was an exceptionally calm and collected person. He was the kind of man who never seemed to lose himself in any situation. A single rupee or a million simply made no difference to him. Observing his dignified lifestyle, his considerate interaction with people and his depth of thought was enough to tell me what I should and should not do in life. He was and remains my beacon. He always said, 'Never let success go to your head or failure to get you down.' If I can inculcate even 50 per cent of his way of living into the rest of my life, I will have achieved something in life!
>
> —Sachin Tendulkar, *Cricket Today*, May 2005

Sachin's comrade-in-arms in the Shardashram team was Vinod Kambli, a destructive left-handed batsman. A lesser coach would have allowed his wards to feast on weak bowling attacks, but Achrekar loathed this approach. A long-term thinker, he ensured that the boys played against older cricketers on a regular basis. Both Sachin and Vinod were good enough to make the adjustments and succeed, much to the consternation of their opponents. When their coach sought to test their fortitude, the pupils responded by testing his patience, as was proved by the number of the times he had to physically drag them out of the nets; the boys simply wanted to bat, bat and bat.

> To achieve your dream, you have got to chase it hard. There will be obstacles and hurdles along the way, but keep pushing yourself hard. [On] a number of occasions, we push ourselves hard and then turn back, thinking that we have tried and it hasn't worked. However, success is waiting for you [just] around the corner. Don't give up. Passion allows you to push yourself harder... Just find a reason to wake up in the morning and chase your dreams.
>
> —Sachin Tendulkar (Speech), 50th Inter IIT Sports Meet, December 2014

A mountain of runs in the 1985–86 and 1986–87 seasons ensured Sachin's inclusion in the Mumbai Ranji Trophy squad for the 1987–88 season. He was only fourteen at the time. Although he did not play a single game, he keenly observed his seniors on the field and listened to them off it. He could have 'taken it easy', having realized that the star-studded Mumbai team was strong enough to have no room for him in its playing XI, but he chose to learn as much as he could during his stint on the bench.

He was awarded his 'Mumbai Cap' in the Ranji Trophy West Zone league game against Gujarat in the next season. This was shortly after Dilip Vengsarkar, his Mumbai and India senior and the then captain of the national team, got him to bat against the best bowlers in the country, including a certain Kapil Dev.

Sachin scored a century in his very first Ranji outing and followed it with knocks of 58 and 89 against Saurashtra on a Rajkot wicket where the ball was turning square. He was Mumbai's highest scorer in the 1988–89 season. He was even touted as a likely pick for India's tour of the West Indies in early 1989, but the selectors left him out.

Six months later, the selection panel met in Mumbai to pick the Indian team for a Pakistan tour. Three of the five members were in favour of his inclusion. Most importantly, one of them was Raj Singh Dungarpur, who chaired the committee.

At the age of sixteen years and 205 days, Sachin Tendulkar was India's 187th Test cricketer and the youngest ever, when he took the field with his teammates at the National Stadium, Karachi, Pakistan, on 15 November 1989. Batting first, Pakistan scored 409. India was in more than a spot of bother at 41–4 on the second day, when Sachin came in for the first time in a Test match as a batsman. He got off the mark in Test cricket with a boundary, but the experience of facing the Pakistani pacemen left him shaken. Post his dismissal after scoring 15 runs, he admitted to his teammates that he had 'been in a hurry'.

However, there was a silver lining. He may have panicked internally, but he had displayed equanimity externally during his stay in the middle. The sixteen-year-old had inadvertently demonstrated how to come across in a crisis; you might be feeling lost or may even be broken internally, but never show it. When the dust settles down and the world takes stock of what has happened, it is your composure that will be remembered. The respect that others have for you will rise by several notches, and even your self-belief will be enhanced, because you will start feeling that if you can come across as cool and unruffled in a situation like that, then you can handle just about anything that comes your way.

LEARNING TIP

Even if you are diffident, never show it.
Instead, focus on the task at hand.
That will eventually enhance your self-belief.

This is exactly what happened in Sachin's case. Among those who witnessed Sachin's straight drive that got him off the mark in Test cricket was Abdul Qadir, one of the greatest leg-spinners of all time and an individual adept at reading batsmen's minds. Even he was 'deceived' by Sachin's display of equanimity, and he went so far as to say that he sensed something 'special' about Sachin's poise and body language!

Achrekar's emphasis on match-practice and exposing his pupils to different situations had paid off.

The temperament that Sachin had acquired and honed under the tutelage of his Guru, manifested itself on the eve of the second Test at Faisalabad. The teenager, who was convinced after his first Test innings that he would never ever play Test cricket again, trained hard in the nets and concentrated on quickening his movements to bring them in sync with the demands of international cricket.

He had recognized the need to 'respect' the format and those whom he had been pitted against; this was Test cricket—the apogee of the sport, and not an inter-school game. Sachin decided to look at the clock, not the scoreboard, and made up his mind to bat in half-hour instalments. At Faisalabad, he made it through the first thirty minutes and felt different. He felt that he had it in him to come to terms with Test cricket.

The outcome was an innings of 59, his first fifty at the highest level. He went in at 101–4 and helped India reach 288.

India had started the four-Test series as underdogs, but solid batting and incisive bowling enabled them to thwart their opponents in the first three Tests. The Pakistanis dished out a 'green-top' for the final Test at Sialkot, ostensibly to favour their own quicks, but the move nearly backfired as India took a first-innings lead of 74. Then, there was a twist in the tale. Pakistan made early dents in the second innings and reduced India to 38–4. India were ahead by only 112 with just six wickets in hand, and all the senior batsmen were back in the pavilion, with the exception of Navjot Sidhu. He was joined in the middle by the teenager. With more than a day's play left, the Indians had their backs to the wall.

Sachin had just about got in when Waqar Younis, another player who had made his Test debut at Karachi, steamed in at him and let one go that reared off the pitch after landing just short of a length. The cherry struck Sachin on his helmet and ricocheted off it onto his nose, even before he could react.

As the injured batsman reeled from the impact and felt the blood trickling down his chin, he was surrounded by Sidhu and nearly the entire Pakistani team. Members of the home team advised that he leave the field for medical attention. Their concern was, of course, laced with gamesmanship. They knew, as did Sachin, that his departure would take them that bit closer to attacking the Indian lower order.

For Sachin, it was 1984 all over again. Back then, his family had left the final call on his cricketing future to him, and he had decided to leave his comfort zone and shift to Shardashram. At Sialkot, it was again up to him to take the final call. He asked Salil Ankola, the 12th man, to apply ice on the wound. He then wiped the blood with a towel and informed the gathering that he intended to carry on.

His coach had stressed the importance of being fearless and taking blows, if any, in one's stride. The pupil had not forgotten.

Waqar figured that his opponent might expect another bouncer; he accordingly decided to do just the opposite. He bowled a delivery that was fuller, but Sachin had read his mind to perfection. The batsman advanced his front foot purposefully and met the ball with the full face of his bat. His timing and placement were impeccable and the red cherry whizzed through the covers for four. Sachin went on to score 57, his second fifty in the series, and added 101 with Sidhu. India were 234–7 at the end of the game, and the series ended in a 0-0 stalemate. For the Indians, drawing a Test series against a formidable Pakistani team on its own soil was akin to victory.

> It was hard for the senior players to mix around with me in Pakistan. I was only sixteen then. I don't think anyone was awestruck by my presence. Perhaps they were, when I did not come back after getting hit... My teammates thought I would come back because my nose was bleeding... When I got back [after the partnership], I could make out that everybody felt happy that I stayed there.
>
> —Sachin Tendulkar, *The Sportstar*, 6 May 1995

In December 1989, a sixteen-year-old proved to his teammates, all of whom were much senior to him in terms of age and experience, that age was just a number.

LEARNING TIP

How well you acquit yourself when confronted by a crisis, matters. How old you are when you are confronted by one, does not.

When it comes to crisis management, a direct parallel can be drawn between the teenaged Sachin and Lord Krishna, one of Hinduism's most popular and revered deities. Krishna was a child prodigy who never allowed his age to come in the way of assuming responsibility, standing up for the good and taking on the forces of evil, and inspiring others in the process.

This was in tune with what Sachin did throughout his career. He concentrated on doing what was within his control to the best of his abilities. Never did he fret over things that were beyond his control.

Sachin Ramesh Tendulkar possessed the desire to excel as a cricketer. Even at the age of sixteen, he was obsessed with the four Ds—Devotion, Dedication, Discipline and Determination. Everything else was uncontrollable and not worth wasting time on. To paraphrase Gary Player, the celebrated golfer, 'the harder Sachin prepared, the luckier he got.' The calls he took in mid-1984 and at Sialkot in late 1989 changed his life—and Indian cricket's—for good.

LEARNING TIP

Better to concentrate on doing that which is within your control, rather than fret over things that are beyond your control.

2

Be a Quick Learner

The Tendulkar Way

I saw him playing on the television and I was very, very struck by his technique. I asked my wife to come and have a look at him. Because, I said, I never saw myself play, but I feel that this fellow is playing much the same as I used to play. She had a look at him on the television and she said, 'Yes, there is a similarity between the two.' It was just his compactness, his stroke production, his technique…it all seemed to gel as far as I was concerned.

—Sir Donald Bradman on Sachin Tendulkar

The greatest batsman of all time had followed Sachin's progress from the time the he had toured Australia as an eighteen-year-old in 1991–92. The astute individual that 'the Don' was, it will be safe to say that there was a lot left unsaid when he explained why Sachin reminded him of himself, in the mid-1990s. The two men had a lot more in common than tangible aspects. Both were quick learners, for instance.

India's next assignments after the series against Pakistan in late 1989 were tours of New Zealand and England. The national team saw quite a few departures, arrivals and comebacks during this phase. K. Srikkanth, who had led the team in Pakistan, was not picked for the New Zealand tour and the reins were entrusted to Mohammed Azharuddin.

Sachin lived up to his reputation in both New Zealand and England, but far more impressive than the scores he registered was his proficiency at learning from his mistakes. Indeed, this was a trait he displayed to perfection for the remainder of his career.

In the fields of sport and entertainment, there have been numerous instances of teenage prodigies failing to live up to expectations. Those among them who have fallen by the wayside have been generally undone by their blatant defiance of authority and convention, mostly in a negative rather than constructive way, a proclivity to think no end of themselves and shoot their mouths off at the slightest opportunity, their indulgence in different kinds of abuse, ranging from substance to sexual, or a combination of all these transgressions and more.

The teenaged Sachin Tendulkar personified the antithesis of this template. He was assured, never arrogant. As the late Ashok Mankad, a former Test cricketer and renowned coach, put it, 'He was not arrogant, but his talent was arrogant.'

The teenager's assurance was palpable when he told Tom Alter, the actor and TV anchor, in an interview recorded in early 1989 that he would have handled the West Indies fast bowlers, had he been picked for the tour of the Caribbean that the Indian team was scheduled to undertake. This was a time when the West Indies were invincible in Test cricket and their fast bowlers were dreaded by batsmen the world over. The teenager was not bragging; he meant what he said.

LEARNING TIP

Arrogance and assurance are not synonymous.
Avoid the former and embrace the latter.

He already held the distinction of being India's youngest Test cricketer ever; in the second Test of the New Zealand series at Napier, it appeared as if he would achieve another honour—of being the youngest centurion in Test cricket. The record then stood in the name of Pakistan's Mushtaq Mohammed, who had reached triple figures against India at Delhi in 1960–61 at the age of seventeen years and 82 days.

Sachin spent a lot of time in the nets after failing in the first Test at Christchurch. His determination to improve upon his first-ball duck and 24 in the first Test was reflected in the way he handled the New Zealand bowlers on the third day of the Napier Test. He batted with aplomb to reach a score of 80 by the time stumps were drawn. Followers of Indian cricket and the teenager himself could not wait for the game to resume the next day.

He got going on day four with two boundaries off Danny Morrison, the spearhead of New Zealand's pace attack. The bowler, a seasoned campaigner, put himself in his opponent's shoes to try and anticipate his next move. Sachin had done likewise after being hit on the nose by Waqar Younis at Sialkot, but this time around, he did not. He was probably distracted, because the international cricketer within him was engaged in a bout with the teenager within him. The batsman who had scored mountains of runs for his school, excelled in his first full season as a first-class cricketer and then impressed in his first international series, had had the better of the bowler till that point. However, with the landmark only 12 runs away, the batsman let his guard drop and gave the teenager an opening. The teenager's knockout punch came in the form of an impetuous stroke to a well-disguised slower delivery by Morrison. The paceman was convinced that the batsman would attempt another aggressive stroke, and he was right. Sachin's timing went horribly awry and the ball flew off the bat to John Wright, who was standing at mid-off. The catch was held with ease and Sachin left the ground in tears. An error in judgement had cost the 'boy wonder' a world record.

Having never been the sort to brood over his mistakes,

Sachin got over the disappointment and focused on the challenges ahead.

The first Test of the series against England, played at Lord's—the 'Mecca of Cricket,' was a disappointment for the Indian team and a mixed bag for Sachin. He pulled off an incredible one-handed catch to dismiss Allan Lamb, one of England's batting spearheads, but could not get going with the bat. Scores of 10 and 27 prompted him to seek the advice of his seniors.

Sunil Gavaskar, his childhood hero and the greatest opening batsman of all time, was only too happy to extend a helping hand. He told Sachin to 'wait for the ball to come to him rather than reach out for the ball.' The lessons that Sachin had learnt at Karachi and Napier about respecting the format, opposition and conditions, were refreshed.

The 'quick learner' in him was visible in the second Test at Old Trafford, Manchester. In the first innings, he dropped anchor and negotiated everything that was hurled at him with poise and patience. After forty-nine minutes at the crease, he received a delivery from Michael Atherton that begged to be cut; Sachin obliged by dispatching it for four. Those were his first runs.

Not scoring a run for forty-nine minutes was out-of-character for him, but that did not deter Sachin from striving to surprise himself. In the process, he surprised the world, especially those who still considered him a 'tearaway' batsman.

He went on to score 68 and returned to the pavilion,

a far better batsman than he had ever been at any stage of his brief career. In the second innings, he went several steps further. India needed to bat out the last five sessions of the game to save the match; the target of 408 that England had set for them was purely academic. However, the senior members of the batting line-up, some of whom had excelled in the first innings, buckled under the pressure. At 127–5 and with a lot of time left, another defeat loomed large for the visiting team.

Sachin carried on from where he had left off in the first innings. He had a stroke of luck when Eddie Hemmings, the off-spinner, floored a return catch. The batsman blanked out the 'life' from his memory and goaded himself to concentrate harder. Fortune was favouring the brave, and the harder he was applying himself to the task at hand, the luckier he was getting, it appeared. Sachin was supported by Manoj Prabhakar, who came in at no. 8 and dropped anchor at the other end. The spectators went into raptures when the teenager drove Angus Fraser for three to complete his maiden Test century. He was only seventeen years and 112 days old. The match ended in a draw and Sachin was clapped off the ground by his opponents, many of whom had been playing first-class cricket for years even before the 'boy-wonder' had joined Achrekar's nets at Shivaji Park in 1984.

> I was sitting in the lounge, after breakfast (on the morning after the Test ended). He came over. There was space on the sofa on which I was sitting, but he did not sit there. He sat on the ground, at my feet, and

> asked, 'Sir, how did I play? Did I commit any mistakes?' A teenager who scored his first Test century against England in England should have been flying high, but he wasn't. I told him that any cricketer would have been proud to have played an innings like that. What was important was his urge to learn.
>
> —Madhav Mantri (Manager, Indian cricket team to England, 1990), *Million Dollar Babies*, Star Cricket, 2008

Sachin was deeply respectful of his seniors and never considered himself bigger than the sport.

He played eleven Test matches in four countries in his first year of international cricket—four in Pakistan, three in New Zealand, three in England and one in India. They taught him to plan, to be patient and to bide his time. He applied everything that he had learnt in his first year on India's Australia tour in 1991–92, a watershed in his career. Some of his colleagues oozed confidence that was bordering on arrogance in their interactions with the media on the eve of their departure, leaving no one in doubt that they expected to be successful in the contests to follow. On the other hand, Sachin was the epitome of assurance. When his views were sought, he simply said that he had watched footage of matches in Australia and thought that he could do 'fairly well'.

Like his teammates, Sachin looked all at sea in the first Test at Brisbane. The juice in the wickets and the bounce that the Australian bowlers were extracting from the strips seemed almost unreal to batsmen who were used to the 'slow and low' strips of the subcontinent. In the second Test at Melbourne, he batted for two hours and hit five fours in a knock of 40, before playing an injudicious stroke off Peter Taylor, the off-spinner. The ball gathered more height than distance and Allan Border ran several yards to take the catch. Sachin was cross with himself for having got himself out. He figured that if he were to channelize his aggression constructively, there was no reason why he could not have a longer outing in the middle.

Ironically, most of his batting colleagues were not looking 'out of form' in the strictest sense of the term. They would get off to starts and look untroubled. However, they were not getting many scoring opportunities. The Australian bowlers, backed by their fielders, were good enough to ensure that the first mistake made by a batsman was his last. They had forced the Indian batsmen to go on the defensive, technically as well as mentally, so much so that the latter were finding it difficult to even capitalize on the rare loose delivery. A vicious circle was completed by the 'scoreboard pressure', which kept increasing because of the batsmen's failure to make the bad balls count and forced them to make mistakes.

The Australians soon found out that the youngest member of the Indian team was immune to the 'scoreboard pressure'. Sachin, they discovered, was proficient at picking runs off not only the bad balls, but also some good ones. That the team had come to depend on him, brought out the best in him.

> Once we reached Australia, I realized that this was a different ball game altogether. I quickly got adjusted to the pace and bounce.
>
> —Sachin Tendulkar, *Thank You Sachin*, BCCI, 2013

He scored an unbeaten 148 in the game and followed it with an exceptional 114 in the fifth Test at Perth. By the time the series ended with India losing 0–4, the youngest player and quickest learner in the Indian batting line-up had become its mainstay. It was a tag he would not relinquish for the next twenty-two years.

Subsequently, Sachin scored two more Test hundreds at the Sydney Cricket Ground. His unbeaten 241 in the last Test of the 2003–04 series is an innings that will be remembered for years to come. He had not done well with the bat in the preceding three Tests of the series. The Australian bowlers had carried out a sustained and disciplined attack on the line of the off-stump or just outside it, whenever he was on strike, and they had largely been successful in blunting him. Three years previously, a run of ordinary scores by Sachin would have spelt disaster for the team, but things were different in the new millennium. The likes of Rahul Dravid, V.V.S. Laxman, Virender Sehwag and Sourav Ganguly had come into their own and they had compensated for their senior teammate's failure to get going. To say that Sachin was 'overdue' for a big one as the final Test approached was an understatement.

His response to the situation was to forget that he

possessed one of the best cover drives in the game's history. The stroke had led to his downfall earlier in the series, with the Australian bowlers finding the outside-edge of his bat. Sachin was too good an exponent of the cover drive to keep mistiming the stroke, but at Sydney, he was determined not to give the opposition even a whiff of a chance. The man who could have essayed the cover drive with his eyes closed, eschewed the stroke totally. He batted for 613 minutes and steered his team towards a mammoth score. Of his 241 runs, only 54 were scored on the off-side.

In compiling that innings in the first week of 2004, Sachin defied twelve men—eleven Australians and himself—to achieve something that was nothing short of superhuman. He did not hesitate to leave his comfort zone to make a statement, when the same was demanded of him.

LEARNING TIP

Leaving your comfort zone may seem a daunting proposition, but it will only enhance the chances of you becoming a more rounded professional.

Among the many lessons imparted by senior members of Marathi middle-class families to their children is that 'while failure was not a crime, aiming low was definitely one.' Sachin, a product of a middle-class family himself, had imbibed and internalized this dictum at a very early age.

The teenager with an impulsive streak evolved into an

adult who lived in the present but had long-term goals. Like champions in every vocation, he always thought 'long-term' and did not mind taking a backward step or two if it took him closer to his long-term objective. This was in stark contrast to people who epitomize mediocrity, in that they are concerned only with short-term gains and not inclined to exert themselves to scale higher peaks.

LEARNING TIP

While failure is not a crime,
aiming low definitely is.

Think Long-term

Sachin's penchant for thinking of the bigger picture has a parallel in military history. One of the reasons India was trounced by the Chinese in the war of 1962 was because the army was caught napping. Our soldiers were pushed into the conflict without getting the requisite time to prepare and acclimatize. Nearly a decade later, General Sam Manekshaw, Chief of Staff of the Indian Army, was determined not to repeat the blunders committed by those who had called the shots in 1962. When advised in April 1971 to invade the then East Pakistan, the General responded with a dead bat, in cricketing terms. He emphasized the need to ensure that the army was fully prepared and in position before any military action was initiated. The Himalayan passes would close only in the winter, thus significantly reducing the chances of Pakistan's all-weather friend forcing India to fight on two fronts. The General also drew the PM's attention to the fact that a military campaign in East Pakistan during the monsoon was doomed to be a disaster, as the inundation would hamper the movement of troops. The Prime Minister saw the merit in the General's arguments. The outcome was a resounding military victory for India in December that year.

No treatise on Sachin Tendulkar would be complete without a mention of his heroics against Australia in back-to-back games of a tri-series in Sharjah, UAE, in April 1998. In the last league game, the Indian team were set a target of 285 by the Australians, who had already qualified for the final. However, quite a few people were 'aiming low' and eyeing a smaller figure—254. This was the number of runs India needed to score to get ahead of New Zealand, the third team in the fray, in the points table. If they could get to 254, then they would play Australia in the final, regardless of the result of the ongoing game.

Sachin got off to a fine start and he was complemented well by his co-opener Sourav Ganguly and then Nayan Mongia, who came in at number 3, but the innings stumbled in the middle overs. India were 143–4 at the end of the 31st over when a sandstorm interrupted the proceedings. Play was held up for forty-five minutes and the target was revised. India now had 15 overs to score 133 *to win*. A required run rate of nearly 9 per over was intimidating in the pre-Twenty20 era, but what looked obtainable was the number of runs they needed to qualify for the final—94.

Sachin was assertive after the resumption, finding the gaps and running hard between the wickets. The stadium rose to him when he completed a century. When Steve Waugh, the Australian captain, commenced the 42nd over of the innings, India needed 63 runs *to win* from 30 balls. But far more important for most people was the fact that they needed only 24 more *to qualify for the final*. Surely, Sachin would not take it easy now. However, what happened off the first two balls of the over blew their minds. Sachin slapped the first ball on the up, straight into the sightscreen. The next ball, he slammed in the deep, and not only did Damien Martyn miss a catch after getting his hands to the ball, but he also let it go for four runs. It was then that people realized what they had missed all along. Sachin was playing for a win, not to merely qualify!

Waugh's over yielded as many as 15 runs and Sachin kept the strike. The first ball of the next over, bowled by Damien Fleming, was a slower one that Sachin picked early, made room on the leg-side and deposited over the long-on boundary. It was his sixth six. By this time, qualifying had ceased to matter; what mattered was that India needed 42 from 23 balls *to win*.

A flicked two to deep square-leg in the same over enabled India to reach the 'qualification' mark, with 20 deliveries to spare. With 32 needed to win from 19 balls, Sachin was caught behind, and the Australians tightened the screws to emerge victorious.

The same sides took the field for the final two days later. Once again, the Australians set India a stiff target, but this time around, the Indians won. Leading the charge was Sachin Tendulkar, who on his 25th birthday followed his score of 143 in the last league game with an incredible innings of 134 in the final.

Sachin's approach in the encounter that is remembered today as the 'Sandstorm Game' could be interpreted as an illustration of his penchant for aiming high. He believed in keeping his mind uncluttered and focussing on positive goals, instead of worrying about negative possibilities.

However, this did not mean that he was closed to opting for discretion over valour when circumstances dictated the same.

LEARNING TIP

Believe in long-term results more than short-term gains.

Looking at the Bigger Picture

The Indian team was playing against Pakistan in a league game of the Asia Cup in Colombo, Sri Lanka six years after the 'Sandstorm Game' in Sharjah. Up against a target of 301, the Indians kept losing wickets at regular intervals, even as Sachin carried on at the other end. When the fifth wicket went down with 151 runs on the board, a further 150 were needed from 127 deliveries. Sachin had the option of taking the bull by the horns. He was of course capable of taking his team through, but there was always the risk of his getting out. Unlike Sharjah in April 1998, India had one league game left in the competition and there was a possibility of their qualifying for the final, provided they won that. However, they would first need to deny Pakistan a bonus point in the ongoing game. If Pakistan were to win with a bonus point, then India would be out of the race even before their last league encounter.

Sachin assessed the situation and revised his approach. There was a method in his malleability. He set his sights on the mark of 241, the score India had to reach to deny their traditional rivals the bonus point. His approach did not delight the jingoists who perceive matches against Pakistan as a variation of war, but what mattered to Sachin was to keep his team afloat in the tournament. He was dismissed for 78, but the lower order took a cue from what he had initiated and ensured that India reached the 241-run mark. Pakistan won the game, but without a bonus point. India went on to beat Sri Lanka in their last league game and qualified for the final at Pakistan's expense. The final was an anti-climax for Indian supporters, with Sri Lanka avenging their loss in the last league game.

A parallel could be drawn between what Sachin did in the Asia Cup game against Pakistan and something that Shivaji, the Maratha warrior-king who took on the Mughals, did in the mid-1660s.

Just as Shivaji never gave his foes the time and space to regroup, Sachin was known to take many a match away from the opposition with his brilliance. However, both were anything but stubborn. They were open to compromising whenever circumstances necessitated the same. Aurangzeb, the Mughal Emperor, dispatched Mirza Jai Singh and Diler Khan—two of his most experienced generals, to attack Shivaji, in 1665. The Marathas suffered heavy losses and Shivaji decided to back off. He assessed the situation and figured that if he were to continue the battle, then his kingdom and all those who lived in it were at the risk of being overrun and annihilated by the Mughal hordes. He wasn't very happy about giving the Mughals the impression that their military might have forced him to cease hostilities, but the visionary in him was looking at the broader picture. He did not want to undo everything that his people, who swore by him and his dream of 'Hindavi Swarajya', had worked so hard to achieve, just to boost his own ego. A short-term compromise was a pragmatic option in the circumstances. When Aurangzeb invited him to Agra, Shivaji decided to go, despite knowing that the Mughal Emperor could not be trusted. However, the Maratha king was prepared to risk himself, but not his subjects. Not surprisingly, Aurangzeb placed him under house arrest. Shivaji proceeded to stage an audacious escape, following which, he took his time to reorganize and rebuild his forces. He then reconquered the forts and territory that he had been forced to cede to the Mughals and laid the foundation of the Maratha Empire.

The Asia Cup game wasn't the only time Sachin had viewed the bigger picture. His innings of 95 against the same team at Lahore, Pakistan, in 2005–06 was a classic. Pakistan won the first ODI of a five-match series and India hit back with a victory in the second. Thus, the traditional rivals had everything to play for in the third encounter at Lahore's Gaddafi Stadium. A target of 289 looked insurmountable when Virender Sehwag and Irfan Pathan fell with only 12 runs on the board. Their nemesis was Mohammed Asif, Pakistan's pace spearhead, who was making the ball talk on a lively track. Sachin used his experience to get the better of the situation. He negotiated everything that Asif hurled at him and ensured that the scoreboard was kept ticking with singles and twos.

Eventually, Asif's captain chose to give him a breather. This was the opportunity Sachin was waiting for. He knew that the other bowlers were not in Asif's class and would therefore not be able to capitalize on the conditions as well as he had.

Sachin's doggedness in hostile circumstances enabled him to step on the accelerator when the intensity of the opposition abated. He put his team in the driver's seat and gave the likes of Mahendra Singh Dhoni and Yuvraj Singh the licence to be pugnacious. The complexion of the game had changed beyond recognition by the time Asif was brought back, and India overhauled the target with more than 2 overs to spare.

Many theories have and can be advanced to explain why Sachin Tendulkar achieved what he did as a professional cricketer. His willingness to learn from his mistakes and to do everything that was within his control to not repeat them count amongst the most critical ones.

3

Be a Team Player

The Tendulkar Way

Sachin was hurt after being told by (Coach Greg) Chappell that he ought to bat at number four 'in the interests of the team'. The point he made to me was that he had served Indian cricket to the best of his abilities for nearly twenty years and he did not need a Greg Chappell to tell him about 'team interest'; he understood and appreciated it better than most people.

—Professor R.S. Shetty, General Manager, Game Development, BCCI, in a personal interview to the author for *HERO: A Biography of Sachin Tendulkar.*

Sachin Tendulkar was a master at rising to the occasion and delivering in any way possible—be it with the bat, or with the ball, or in the field. He often went a step further, creating opportunities to prove himself when none presented itself.

What happened on the evening of 24 November 1993 is a case in point. India took on South Africa in what was the first-ever day–night game at the Eden Gardens, Kolkata, in the semi-final of a five-nation limited-overs tournament. Batting first, the hosts were bowled out for 195. Mohammed Azharuddin, the captain, top-scored with 90, and Pravin Amre essayed a supporting hand of 48. Sachin, who had had a quiet tournament with the bat, was dismissed for 15. The Indian bowlers then brought their team back into the game with strikes at regular intervals. When the seventh South African wicket fell with 145 runs on the board, it seemed all over for the visitors. However, Anil Kumble, India's premier bowler, had finished his quota of 10 overs, and that was what South Africa's eighth-wicket pair of Brian McMillan and David Richardson capitalized on. The duo attacked India's new-ball pair of Manoj Prabhakar and Javagal Srinath, who had been reintroduced to the attack. The capacity crowd was silenced and the Indian players stunned. With South Africa needing 7 runs from 10 balls and very much in control, Richardson ran himself out, but Indian supporters stayed despondent. The opposition could still get the runs in singles, after all. One run off the remainder of the penultimate over brought the equation down to 6 runs off 6 deliveries. Most critically from the point of view of both sides, McMillan was on strike.

On the field, Mohammed Azharuddin assessed his options. He received a message from Ajit Wadekar, the cricket manager, that Kapil Dev, the most experienced bowler in the team, be assigned the ball. An animated discussion ensued among Azharuddin, Kapil Dev, Ajay Jadeja and Sachin Tendulkar, the vice-captain. It ended with Kapil Dev walking away and Azharuddin handing over the ball to his deputy.

The TV commentators were as incredulous as the spectators and TV viewers when they saw Sachin marking out his run-up and setting his field with a purposeful expression on his face. It was a situation that the bravest of cricketers and individuals would have shied away from. He had not bowled earlier in the game and he had not done anything significant with the bat in the tournament. It would have been easier for him to have joined his captain in convincing Kapil Dev to bowl. The other options were speedsters Javagal Srinath and Salil Ankola, as well as Ajay Jadeja, who had bowled his military medium-pacers well to take 2–31 from nine overs.

Sachin's fans feared for the brickbats that would be tossed at him if he were to fail. However, Sachin himself was not even contemplating that prospect.

The prospect of contributing in any which way to take his team through to the final, fired him up.

> ... I said to myself, 'At any cost, we have to win this game.' I had decided to bowl each and every delivery at the stumps. MacMillan needed four runs off the last ball. I decided to bowl a Yorker. We did not want a

> wicket, we were more concerned about preventing runs at that stage.
>
> —Sachin Tendulkar, *The Sportstar*, November 1994

Sachin's body language, as seen on the television, was overwhelmingly aggressive and positive. There was another suicidal run-out off the first ball and McMillan found himself stuck at the non-striker's end. The next three deliveries were dot-balls and Allan Donald managed a single off the fifth. With South Africa needing a boundary off the last ball, Sachin told Vijay Yadav, the wicketkeeper, to retreat from the stumps to the thirty-yard circle, to eliminate the possibility of an inside-edge flying past him to the boundary. As it turned out, McMillan did get an inside-edge, but Yadav had all the time in the world to intercept it. He allowed South Africa to complete a meaningless single. India had won by 2 runs.

Sachin had delivered in a crisis yet again, this time with the ball. India went on to win the tournament, beating the West Indies in the final.

> I firmly believe that if Sachin were over six feet tall and a little more athletic, he would have been the Garry Sobers of the modern era. In fact, it is safe to bet that he would have given Sobers a run for his money
> I am guessing that it is only when he found out in his teens that he won't grow significantly taller that he gave up the ambition of being a fast bowler and decided that it had to be batting that would take him

> to cricketing greatness. Even today, Tendulkar gets more excited when he sees a good fast bowling talent than when he sees a special batting talent… When I used to captain Mumbai, I had to very tactfully separate Tendulkar from a young fast bowler. Sachin just can't hold back from giving advice to a young quickie; the problem is his advice is a bit too complex for most. Also, what he has in mind is often impossible for a rookie fast bowler to produce. I used to feel sorry for him in such situations. It was as if Tendulkar was trying to live his dream of being a great fast bowler through another, more physically gifted, athlete.
>
> —Sanjay Manjrekar,
> *Outlook Special Commemorative Issue*, 2010

Some individuals who are unable to fulfil all their dreams, become bitter. Sachin did not belong to this category.

LEARNING TIP

Make the most of every opportunity that comes your way.

Unflinching Commitment to the Team's Goals

Steve Waugh's Australian team landed in India, the 'Final Frontier' as they called it, for a three-Test series in early 2001. They had won a record fifteen Tests on the trot prior to the series and they were eager to extend the streak on Indian soil, where they had last won a series in 1969–70. Six playing days into the series, and everything seemed to be happening as they had envisaged. They thrashed the hosts in less than three days in the first Test at Mumbai and held all the aces at stumps on day three of the second Test at Kolkata.

Leading by 274 runs at the end of the first innings, Waugh had enforced the follow-on. India batted a lot better in the second essay and the scoreboard read 254–4 at the end of the third day's play. Indian supporters were relieved, not because of the position their side was in, but because their team was not going to lose by an innings. Considering how the game had flowed until then, it was impossible to visualize India avoiding defeat. Sachin had already been dismissed for identical scores of 10 in both the innings and his part in the game was over—as a batsman, that is.

Day four saw the most extraordinary turnaround in the history of Test cricket. V.V.S. Laxman and Rahul Dravid batted throughout the day and a bit of the fifth, and India were able to declare at 657–7. The Australians were set a target of 384, with less than three sessions of play left. That left the visitors, who had spent more than two days in the field, with no option but to play for a draw. They were 3 wickets down at the tea interval. For the Indian supporters, a draw was as good as a victory, considering the state their team had been in on the third day.

Australia lost two quick wickets after tea, and Matthew Hayden was joined in the middle by fellow southpaw Adam

Gilchrist. At this stage, Sourav Ganguly, the Indian captain, asked Sachin to bowl. To those watching, it seemed no more than a temporary change to give the specialist bowlers a breather; Sachin, they expected, would bowl an over or two at the most and the regulars would then be brought back.

However, Sachin himself wasn't quite seeing it that way. He had not done anything substantial in his primary role as a batsman, and he viewed this as an opportunity that fate had presented him with to make a mark in another role.

He decided to bowl leg-breaks and aimed to land the ball in the rough patch created by the footmarks of the bowlers operating from the opposite end. What followed was sensational. He had both Gilchrist and Hayden leg-before, and the spectators couldn't stop cheering. The twin strikes exposed the Australian lower order and India were only 3 wickets away from achieving the improbable.

Sachin wasn't done yet. He had prevailed in most of his on-field duels with Shane Warne, and he was determined to prevail even when the adversaries reversed roles. The greatest batsman of the modern era tested the greatest leg-spinner of all time with a googly, the variation in a leg-spinner's repertoire that 'goes the other way'. Warne of all people did not pick it and was trapped plumb in front. Harbhajan Singh wrapped up the last two wickets and the nation celebrated like there was no tomorrow.

India went on to take the series with a nail-biting victory in the final Test at Chennai. The triumph was set up by a certain S.R. Tendulkar, who scored 125 in the first innings.

While V.V.S. Laxman and Rahul Dravid were India's best batsmen and Harbhajan Singh India's best bowler in the series respectively, Sachin was clearly the most successful 'all-rounder' on either side. He had a critical role to play in one of the greatest fightbacks in the history of the game.

The series win against Australia in March 2001 drew the average Indian cricket-lover, whose faith had been shaken after the match-fixing scandal that rocked the game the previous year, back to his favourite sport. In that sense, bringing Indian cricket back on track after the events of 2000 will remain the most significant contribution of India's leading cricketers of the time.

▪

Grabbing opportunities with both hands, literally!

While Sachin did some remarkable things with the ball, he was at his best in his primary role. It seems unbelievable today that the batsman who holds the world records for the highest number of runs and centuries in ODIs scored a mere 1,758 runs at an average of 30.84 and with a highest individual score of 84, in his first sixty-nine matches. In the early 1990s, Sachin had thought long and hard about opening the batting in the shorter version of the game. With the benefit of hindsight, getting your best batsman to face as many deliveries as possible seems a no-brainer, but this wasn't quite the norm at a time when One-Day cricket was regarded as nothing more than an abbreviated form of multi-day cricket and not a separate entity that necessitated a different mindset, tactics and even players. There had been a few exceptions to the rule of course, like India assigning an 'attacking' role to a pair of spinners in the World Championship of Cricket in 1985, different sides using middle-order or lower-order batsmen as 'pinch-hitters' to catch the opposition unawares and New Zealand giving the new ball to a spinner in the 1992 World Cup. However, the majority believed at the time that measures such as these were far too risky to be employed on a regular basis.

Brian Lara's success at the top of the order in ODIs only boosted Sachin's conviction that he too would click as an opener, if he were to get the opportunity. At the time, he was India's vice-captain and so was an integral part of the team management. He had the option of throwing his weight around, but he did not. To him, that was 'not cricket'.

The Indian team toured New Zealand at the end of the 1993–94 season to play a solitary Test and four ODIs. The Test ended in a draw and New Zealand won the first ODI, which was the 69th game of Sachin's ODI career.

Navjot Sidhu, who opened the batting for India in both forms, woke up with a stiff neck on the morning of the second ODI at Auckland. This left him in no shape to play the game, and that left the Indian team management with no option but to elevate a middle-order batsman to the opening slot. They were already an opener short, with Manoj Prabhakar having flown home injured. Sachin sensed his chance.

The vice-captain requested Mohammed Azharuddin, the captain, and Ajit Wadekar, the cricket manager, that he be allowed to face the new ball. He assured them that he would not ask them for another chance 'if he were to fail'. New Zealand won the toss and batted first, but they were bowled out for a paltry 142.

When India batted, there was bedlam. Sachin's sequence of scoring strokes read 2, 4, 4, 4, 4, 3, 4, 4, 4, 4, 6, 4, 4, 6, 4, 4, 4, 4, 2, 4, 2 and 1. He faced 49 deliveries in all (there were 27 dot balls) and scored 82 runs. Among those who clapped him off the field after he was dismissed, were his batting partner, the incoming batsman, the New Zealand players, the spectators and even the umpires. India's ODI batting line-up, and indeed, the team's very approach to the shorter version of the game, had been altered for good.

A few belligerent innings later, Sachin scored his maiden ODI hundred against Australia at Colombo, in what was his 79th game. He ended his limited-overs career eighteen years later, with a total of 463 matches, an aggregate of 18,426 runs, an average of 44.83 and a tally of 49 centuries. At least a couple of these figures—if not all—might well stand the test of time.

Sachin's proclivity to make the most of the opportunities that came his way was not restricted to the ones that he actively sought. There were times when he was not entirely happy with the circumstances he found himself in, but he still gave it his best shot for his team. This is the hallmark of a true professional.

His cricketing commitments had made him spend a substantial amount of time away from home since he was fourteen years old. As the years passed, he missed out on quality time with his family. Arjun, his son, would be so upset with Sachin's frequent absences that he would not even speak to him on phone. The father, deeply disturbed, would tell Anjali, his wife, to request Arjun to at least say 'Hello' to him.

However, Sachin never allowed personal worries to get in the way of his professional responsibilities.

His commitment to the team was evident from his very first international series, even before the Sialkot Test where he braved a nose injury to essay a match-saving 57. He arrived at the wicket in the second innings of the second Test at Faisalabad, brimming with confidence after having scored 59 in the first essay. However, his partner in the middle was anything but assured; Mohammed Azharuddin, who had played the first Test at Karachi only because of an injury to Raman Lamba and had scored a duck in the first innings of the ongoing game, was batting for his career.

Azharuddin batted with elegance and maturity until he entered the 90s in a Test for the first time in three years. An attack of nerves resulted in communication issues and a mix-up. It was Sachin who sacrificed his wicket by running to the danger end. A grateful Azharuddin went on to complete his century. A few days after the tour ended, the same batsman who was one of the last players to be picked for the tour of Pakistan was named captain of the Indian cricket team.

Sachin may have been the 'baby' of the team until then,

but that did not get in the way of his helping a teammate who was under pressure. It was a team sport, after all.

▪

Exactly a decade later, Sachin concocted a unique stratagem to bail himself and his partner out of a tight situation. New Zealand were in the driver's seat in a Test match at Mohali, having taken a first-innings lead of 132. The onus was on Sachin and Rahul Dravid, India's top two batsmen, to bring their side back into the game. However, both found themselves struggling against Chris Cairns, who was generating reverse-swing that they were finding hard to pick.

Sachin then suggested to his partner, a right-handed batsman like himself, that whoever was the non-striker between the two of them ought to try to spot what Cairns was trying to do, as he ran in to bowl. If he had held the shiny side on the inside, it would mean that the ball would swing into the striker, and if he were holding the shiny side outside, then the ball would move away from the batsman. The non-striker would hold his bat with his right hand if he reckoned the ball would come in and hold it with his left if he felt it would move away. The ploy worked and the duo settled in to add 229 runs for the third wicket. Rahul scored 144 and Sachin remained unbeaten on 126. There was a point during the stand when Cairns realized what the batsmen were doing. He, therefore, resorted to gripping the ball across the seam and hiding it from the view of the non-striker with his left palm. What he did not know was that the batsmen had decided that the non-striker would hold his bat with both hands if he had no idea how the ball was going to behave! This was teamwork at its best.

India's top two batsmen of the 2000s were asked to do the team a favour in May 2002, when the planning started for the ICC Cricket World Cup 2003. Rahul Dravid was requested to keep wicket in ODIs to lend balance to the team and enable the inclusion of as many as seven specialist batsmen in the playing XI, and Sachin's job description was changed from 'opening aggressor' to 'mid-innings stabilizer'. The hugely successful top-order alliance between Sourav Ganguly and Sachin was terminated, with Virender Sehwag, a disciple of the Tendulkar school of belligerence, moving up to the opening slot.

Sachin gave in because that was what the team wanted him to do. He essayed his new role to perfection, starting with the bilateral series against the West Indies and moving on to a tri-series against England and Sri Lanka, both of which India won. He continued to bat in the middle-order in ODIs till the end of the New Zealand tour in early 2003, after which he was restored to his favourite opening slot for the World Cup.

A year after the 2003 World Cup, Sachin and Rahul Dravid were the protagonists in an episode that could have derailed the Indian cricket team and with it, Indian cricket itself. What threatened to become a clash of personalities and split the team vertically was handled and defused with maturity and tact.

On the second afternoon of the Multan Test against Pakistan, India were sitting pretty at 675–4, with Sachin only 6 runs short of what would have been his second double century on the trot. He had scored an unbeaten 241 in India's previous Test at Sydney. However, he and all those who were waiting to cheer him were shocked when Dravid, who was leading India in the game, declared the innings when Yuvraj Singh was dismissed. There was an hour's play left and the Indian captain wanted to give his bowlers the opportunity to bowl as many deliveries as possible to the Pakistani batsmen, who had fielded for more than ten hours. Sachin knew of his captain's plans, but he was under the impression that he would get a few more deliveries to complete his 200.

When asked at the end-of-day media conference if he was disappointed with the timing of the declaration, Sachin replied in the affirmative. Across the subcontinent and beyond, opinions were sharply divided. While some complimented Dravid for 'putting team above self,' others felt that he could have waited for an over or two.

Dravid decided to be upfront, and so did Sachin. They spoke to each other and reiterated their respective viewpoints, the following morning. They recognized the fact that while there were bound to be disagreements in every relationship, be it personal or professional, it was necessary to forget them for the greater good. The discussion ended with Sachin clarifying that his commitment to his side would in no way be affected by what had happened. Rahul threw the ball to him in the closing stages of the third day, at a time when the Pakistani innings was tottering in response to India's gigantic score. Sachin grabbed the chance to take his team closer to a famous first Test victory on Pakistani soil.

Moin Khan, Pakistan's wicketkeeper-batsman, had no answer to a prodigious leg-break, which went through the batsman's legs and bowled him. Not many people had seen Sachin that jubilant on a cricket field, not even when he scored match and series-winning centuries for India.

History repeated itself on the eve of the ICC Cricket World Cup 2007, with Sachin having another stint in the middle-order in ODIs. However, the circumstances were less harmonious than they had been four years earlier. The way he handled the crisis that stared him and many of his teammates in the face at the time, was typical of the man.

There was discontent in the Indian dressing-room when the side took on the West Indies and Sri Lanka in back-to-back ODI series, just before the ICC Cricket World Cup 2007. The coach had fallen out with a section of a team and some senior players were not pleased to have their credentials and commitment questioned. However, Sachin did not allow the thoughts that were troubling him to have an adverse impact on his batting. He scored a fifty and then a century in the series against the West Indies and a fifty against Sri Lanka.

The World Cup that followed was a catastrophe, with

India being knocked out in the first round itself. The coach put in his papers and subsequently claimed that he had made up his mind to quit, regardless of how the team fared in the quadrennial event.

The players, who bore the brunt of the nation's anger, bounced back in the months to follow. A victorious tour of Bangladesh was followed by a Test series triumph in England, India's first in the country since 1986. Weeks after the conclusion of the England tour, a 'young' Indian team led by Mahendra Singh Dhoni created history, winning the inaugural ICC World Twenty20.

Sachin was one of the senior players who chose to skip the T20 World Cup. He thus missed out on an opportunity to win a World Champion's medal, but the patience, penance and perseverance that he and his colleagues displayed after the disaster in the Caribbean, stood them in good stead in subsequent years. He excelled himself with the bat in the seasons that followed, helping India win Test series against England, New Zealand, Australia, Sri Lanka and Bangladesh. India topped the ICC Test ranking for the very first time in December 2009. Sachin's consistency with the bat was not restricted to Tests; he produced knocks of 163 against New Zealand and 175 against Australia during this period in limited-overs cricket. In February 2010, he became the first batsman to score a double century in ODIs.

Team India's World Cup triumph on 2 April 2011 marked the culmination of the process of resurrection initiated by

Sachin and his teammates after their first-round exit in the 2007 event.

LEARNING TIP

No matter how hostile one's 'work-environment' is, a professional should do his best to control what is controllable and focus on discharging his duties to the best of his abilities. This approach is guaranteed to yield results, if not in the short-term, then certainly in the long-term.

4

Leading from the Front

The Tendulkar Way

When I state that my favourite captain is Sachin Tendulkar, people always seem to have a questioning look, because if you look at the numbers, perhaps his stint as captain was not the most successful. But believe me, he was a very good captain indeed. He gave the freedom to newcomers which is required to blossom as a player. He had a young team when he became captain… Rahul Dravid, V.V.S. Laxman, myself, Javagal Srinath, Kumble, we were all in the maturing stage and so we couldn't deliver the way the captain wanted us to. But Sachin as a captain definitely defined my international career. He brought me up the order in the ODI format and gave me the opportunity to open the innings with him. It was the turning point of my life as a cricketer.

—Sourav Ganguly, *Sports Illustrated*, May 2013

Every leader is a captain, but not all captains are leaders. Sachin Tendulkar represented India from 1989 to 2013, and formally captained the national side in two separate stints that collectively amounted to two years, during this period. However, it would not be inappropriate to say that he unofficially 'led' Indian cricket for the remaining twenty-two years.

He was appointed captain of Mumbai's Ranji Trophy side at the start of the 1993–94 season. Those were not the best of times for India's cricketing capital. Mumbai was by far the most successful team in the history of the country's premier domestic competition, having won the title thirty times in fifty-nine seasons, but the city had not won the title since 1984–85. Sachin was determined to get things back on track.

He was all for innovation. However, he was also aware that changes, if any, needed to be introduced and perfected while training, before they were implemented in a match.

Sachin sought to replicate his coach's Shardashram model when the players got together at the Wankhede Stadium, their home base, to prepare for the season. He had noticed that the corner of the ground where the practice pitches were situated was not exposed to sunlight. This was because of the way the stands had been constructed. He set out to exploit this structural oddity. The groundstaff was instructed to leave the practice surfaces alone. Consequently, there would be a lot of dew on the pitches when training would start at half-past eight in the morning. The best fast bowlers in the city were given the freedom to make the most of the 'juice' on the tracks and give the batsmen everything they had. This was a departure from the norm of bowlers not making their batting colleagues uncomfortable in the nets.

The batsmen were also given the freedom to tackle the bowlers the way they wished. Sachin thus achieved his objective of simulating match-like situations at practice. That led to some thrilling contests between the bat and ball, with the purveyors of the two skills putting their best foot forward, literally and figuratively. The fielding sessions were as competitive, with every player taking a minimum of a hundred catches daily.

The competitive spirit that had been fostered and nurtured in these sessions spilled over into the season. Mumbai won all its league matches outright. Vadodara were thrashed by an innings and 118 runs, Maharashtra outplayed by 9 wickets, Gujarat thrashed by 10 wickets and Saurashtra trounced by 8 wickets. Sachin missed the knockout stage of the competition as he was on national duty, but his teammates carried on what he had begun and Mumbai ended its eight-season drought with a 9-wicket win over Bengal in the final.

Leading by Example

Sachin had 'led by example' since his schooldays. As he evolved as a cricketer and professional, he picked up newer tricks of the trade and mastered the ability to come up with out-of-the-box manoeuvres that would surprise not only the opposition, but also his own teammates.

He won his first Test as captain against Australia in Delhi in 1996–97, but the euphoria of the Indian supporters was short-lived. Hansie Cronje's South Africans seemed streets ahead of both the Indian and Australian sides in the limited-overs tri-series that followed, in terms of preparation, fitness, strategy and performance. India lost all three league games to South Africa, but the hosts managed to qualify for the final on the strength of two wins over Australia. However, South Africa were the overwhelming favourites on the eve of the summit clash in Mumbai, with not even the most ardent Indian supporter inclined to give his team even an outside chance. However, the Indian captain thought otherwise.

He won the toss and elected to bat. India scored 220–7, with the captain contributing 67 runs. In the field, Sachin defied convention by leaving the deep-point region unmanned. The leg-side was fortified instead. The bowlers, who were told to stick to the basics and bowl to their field, responded brilliantly. The South Africans, confronted with a bowling line-up that was attacking their leg-side and not giving them the room to target the gaps on the off, buckled. The visitors, unbeaten at the league stage, were dismissed at

185 runs and India took the trophy.

> From the moment he addressed the team in the huddle prior to taking the field to the very last ball when Allan Donald was bowled, Tendulkar was an absolutely active, even hyper-active, hands-on captain whether in advising bowlers, running the field placements with great thought or even taking advice at committee meetings. This is one triumph which came with him wholly in charge at the controls.
>
> —R. Mohan, *The Sportstar*, 16 November 1996

▪

Putting Himself In The Opponent's Shoes...

What Sachin did in India's very next game—the first of three Tests against South Africa—took not only his opponents but also his teammates by surprise. This was leadership at its best, thinking on one's feet and motivating the members of one's team to do likewise.

By the time he tossed the coin with Hansie Cronje at Ahmedabad's Sardar Patel (Motera) Stadium on the morning of 20 November 1996, Sachin had played the South Africans enough to have figured out that while they were a disciplined outfit, they had a mechanical streak that they found hard to shed, especially when they were put under pressure. They would work out a plan A meticulously and execute it splendidly. However, they rarely had a plan B to fall back on if the opposition were to launch a spirited riposte to their plan A.

The Ahmedabad Test turned out to be a low-scoring affair, played on a pitch that got lower and more unpredictable as the game progressed. South Africa bowled and fielded well and took a first-innings lead of 21 runs. An innings of 51 by V.V.S. Laxman on his Test debut and the obstinacy of the Indian lower order enabled the hosts to set the visitors a target of 170.

South Africa had nearly two days and all the time in the world to get the runs, but they got off to a disastrous start. Javagal Srinath, India's pace spearhead, struck early and reduced them to 0–2. Gary Kirsten and Hansie Cronje then put on 40 before the left-handed opening batsman, who went on to coach India a decade later, fell to Sunil Joshi's left-arm spin. Even at that stage, Cronje was not unduly perturbed, as he believed that he and his colleagues possessed the nous and technique to counter India's spin threat. Brian McMillan, who replaced Kirsten in the middle, was a good player of spin, as was Cronje himself, along with Jonty Rhodes and David Richardson who were due to come in next. The visitors had covered all their bases, as far as they were concerned.

What they did not know was that the Indian captain had put himself in their shoes. Shortly after McMillan was dismissed by Kumble, Sachin did what the opposition batsmen did not expect him to do. In fact, he took even his own compatriots by surprise.

LEARNING TIP

Think on your feet, try not to be predictable, do what your opponents least expect you to do.

Javagal Srinath, who had taken those two early wickets, was pleasantly surprised to be recalled to the attack. Like the South Africans, he could not see how anybody could believe that fast bowling could be effective on that strip and he had resigned himself to spending the remainder of the game in the outfield. Sachin told him to go flat out in short, attacking bursts. His brief to his fast bowler was to go for the opposition's jugular, but not literally. Sachin impressed upon him that he would be lethal if he were to bowl a fuller length on the deteriorating strip. Bowling short and trying to extract bounce from that wicket would be a waste of time and energy, Srinath was told.

That move by Sachin turned the game. South Africa lost their last 6 wickets for 9 runs, before they realized what had hit them. Srinath scalped four of those to finish with figures of 6–21. India won by 64 runs, and the South African captain admitted that he and his team had been outsmarted.

As a leader, Sachin was prepared to take hard decisions and at the same time take the blame for failures. However, when his moves clicked, as they did at Mumbai and Ahmedabad, he was the first to compliment his teammates. He had no hesitation in taking the rap when his move to promote Robin Singh to number four in an ODI against Pakistan at Sharjah in December 1997, came unstuck, with the left-hander falling for no score.

Mahendra Singh Dhoni, who captained India in different formats of the game from 2007 to 2016, was known to attend post-match media conferences himself, after defeats. He would designate other members of the team, like the Player of the Match or the coach, to interact with the media after wins.

LEARNING TIP

A leader evaluates every possibility and strategizes accordingly. He takes responsibility for failures and credits his colleagues and their respective contributions when the times are good.

Sachin's manoeuvres at Mumbai and Ahmedabad were in the same league as those executed by Keith Mallory, the character portrayed by Gregory Peck in *The Guns of Navarone*. The film is set in 1943, when the Second World War was at its most intense. It starts by informing the audience that 2,000 Allied soldiers are stuck on the island of Kheros off the coast of Turkey. They have run out of supplies and are sitting ducks for the Germans. The Allied High Command learns of the Axis High Command's plans to storm the island in six days' time and in the process bulldoze Turkey, which has stayed neutral till then, to enter the war on its side. The only way the Allies can evacuate the soldiers before the Axis powers attack is by sea. But there is a catch, Allied ships sailing in that corridor of the Aegean Sea are within the range of two German guns that have been installed on the island of Navarone. The Allies, therefore, hatch a desperate plan; a team of saboteurs is dispatched to infiltrate enemy lines to spike the guns before the ships pass by on their way to Kheros.

The mission starts disastrously when Major Roy Franklin, who is in charge, breaks his leg in a fall. Mallory takes over. Matters get progressively worse when the saboteurs receive a message that the Germans are to hit Kheros a day before schedule, which means that they have twenty-four hours less in which to complete their mission. Major Franklin, who is not around when this message is received, tries to kill himself, as he realizes that he is slowing the team down. Mallory then takes the gamble of a lifetime; he lies to the Major that their mission has been aborted. HQ has planned an amphibious assault on Navarone instead and the team's revised brief is to 'create as much disturbance on the island as it can.'

Like a cricket captain trying to put himself in the opposition's shoes and thinking 'two overs ahead' of the proceedings, Captain Mallory works out that he and his team would have to leave Franklin behind at some stage of their mission. While the Major's integrity is beyond question, the Germans would seek to capitalize on the fact that he was wounded. If pushed beyond the pain barrier, he would 'spill the beans'. The Germans would take him seriously and prepare for the amphibious assault that would of course never take place, thus giving the saboteurs a chance to complete the original mission.

The saboteurs leave the Major behind in the town of Mandrakos. Members of the team are shocked to hear Captain Mallory's 'brainwave' when he brings them up to date. Corporal Miller, the explosives expert, whose job it will be to rig the guns, is apoplectic. A close friend of Franklin's, he accuses Mallory of needlessly dragging the Major along till his wounds turned gangrenous, using him like a 'ventriloquist's dummy' and abusing a human life. Mallory defends himself aggressively, although he is aware that what Miller is saying isn't all that far from the truth. The leader that he is, Mallory possesses the tenacity to take tough calls and stand by them. The team always comes first, never the individual.

Mallory's hunch is proved right and everything transpires as he has anticipated. The Major 'spills the beans' to the Germans, and they take positions along the coastline in anticipation of the amphibious assault. By the time they realize that they have been bluffed, it is too late.

Not only does Mallory outsmart the enemy, but he also takes his teammates by surprise. The unfortunate bit is that he is forced to lie to a wounded colleague and inadvertently 'use' an individual to bolster the chances of his team's success.

It is also critical for a leader to know what makes his

teammates tick and how to get the best out of them. Captain Keith Mallory lets Corporal Miller lash out at him, first over his 'mistreatment' of Major Franklin and then after the identity of the 'traitor' in their team has been uncovered. Miller challenges Mallory to shoot the traitor dead and prove that 'he was a father to his men.' Mallory seeks to comply with the request, but Maria, another member of the team, does the deed. She feels more betrayed by the traitor than the others do. This stuns Miller, and Mallory gets an opening. Roles are reversed as he gives Miller a dressing down. 'You are in it now, up to your neck,' he tells the contrite Miller, and all but threatens to kill him if he does not prove that he is the 'genius with explosives' that he is being made out to be. Eventually, Miller optimizes his genius and borrows from the Germans' own arsenal to complete the mission.

The Indian team under Sachin toured South Africa for a full series in the middle of the 1996–97 season, days after beating the same team 2–1 at home. The first Test of the 'return' series at Durban was disastrous for the visitors. They were blown away for 100 in the first innings and 66 in the second, and lost by 328 runs. The silver lining was Rahul Dravid's batting in the second innings. He came in at no. 6 and contributed an unbeaten 27 to India's total of 66. There was something about his technique and temperament that appealed to all those who watched him, the Indian captain included. Sourav Ganguly had done very well at the pivotal no. 3 slot since his Test debut earlier in the year, but Sachin reckoned that the team needed solidity more than flamboyance at the one-drop slot against quality fast bowlers on the lively pitches of South Africa and the West Indies, where they were to tour next. He accordingly made Dravid an offer that the latter could not refuse.

Sixteen years later, Rahul Dravid ended his career with more runs as a 'no. 3'—10,524—than any other batsman in Test cricket history, inclusive of some of the greatest innings ever played.

Sachin's display of leadership outlived his stints as captain of Mumbai and Indian teams. His match-winning double century for Mumbai against Tamil Nadu in the semi-final of the Ranji Trophy in 1999–00 was a veritable masterclass on the art of innings-management as well as man-management.

Mumbai needed to score 486 runs to take the first innings lead. When Ajit Agarkar, the last recognized batsman in the line-up, fell, Mumbai still required 37 runs with 2 wickets in hand. They did achieve their objective, but interestingly, Abey Kuruvilla and Santosh Saxena, the numbers ten and eleven respectively, did not score a single run! Sachin marshalled the chase. As the team got closer to the target, Robin Singh, the Tamil Nadu skipper, dropped all his fielders back to deny Sachin boundaries. The batsman was not flustered. His response was to place the ball in the vacant areas and complete twos quite comfortably. The twos also enabled him to keep the strike. The Tamil Nadu players could not relax, as they were aware that every run that was scored was bringing Mumbai closer to the target. Eventually, the twos forced the fielders to come in. That was the cue for Sachin to take full toll of anything loose and hit boundaries whenever the opportunity presented itself.

> I remember a square-drive that passed within seven yards of Robin [Singh] and he could not stop it... It was a situation where you had to do everything possible to anticipate the opposition's moves. I had seen S. Mahesh, TN's new-ball bowler, delivering a slower ball from 26 yards, earlier in the innings. He had jumped when he was next to the umpire and released the ball from behind the crease. When I saw him do that again, I sensed that another slower ball was on the way and went down the pitch to meet it with the full face of the bat. The ball cleared the roof of the Wankhede at the far end. There was also an interesting battle with Hemang Badani, who was fielding at point. I began altering my stance when I overheard him informing J. Gokulakrishnan, the TN bowler, how I was standing. I would do exactly the opposite of what he had told the bowler, after the latter had started his run-up. This happened 3–4 times and I informed Hemang after the game that unknown to him, I understood a bit of Tamil!
>
> —Sachin Tendulkar, in an MCA volume commemorating Mumbai's 500th Ranji Trophy Match, MCA, 2017

In the same volume, Sachin recalled another of his tactics that worked for the team.

> ...[it] was my deliberate heckling of Ramesh Powar when he came in to bat. As planned with him, I kept telling him within earshot of the fielders to play as straight as possible. Unknown to them, he had been instructed to 'disobey' me and do what he wished. The fielders crowded him, but he managed to get a couple of boundaries with unorthodox shots that landed in the vacant areas of the outfield.
>
> Santosh fell immediately after we had taken the lead. Back in the dressing-room, we reminded each other that we led by only five runs. There was a lot of time left in the game and Tamil Nadu had nothing to lose. We needed to be on our guard. As it turned out, we got them out cheaply and went on to win by 8 wickets.

▪

Sachin's aversion to resting on his laurels did not mean that he was reluctant to celebrate success. His commitment to causes that the world at large may have deemed as insignificant, was exemplary. His double century for Mumbai against Tamil Nadu in 1999–00 was not watched by a capacity crowd. It was a domestic game that not many people, apart from the true connoisseurs, were following. However, the way he celebrated after hitting the boundary that gave Mumbai the first-innings lead, was similar to the way he reacted to the World Cup win in 2011.

The 2000 edition of the ICC Knockout (later rechristened the ICC Champions Trophy), played in Nairobi, Kenya, featured one of Sachin's most memorable mind-games. When he and Sourav Ganguly, the captain, opened for India in a league game against Australia, they had caution in mind. The conditions were overcast and the Australian pacemen were likely to capitalize on the moisture in the wicket and make the ball talk. The Indian openers had, therefore, decided to be watchful. However, a closer look at Glenn McGrath left Sachin in no doubt that if they were to bat the way they had planned, then he would end up bowling the way he wanted to and dent the Indians with early strikes.

Sachin then took it upon himself to do something totally unexpected. The bowler, who never shied away from expressing himself on a cricket field, was stunned to find himself at the receiving end of a verbal barrage from his opponent. Not used to being 'sledged' by the batsman, McGrath first lost his composure and consequently, his focus. He then started targeting the heads of the batsmen rather than their wickets. Sachin was delighted, because he knew McGrath's fuller deliveries would be more lethal than his short deliveries, in those conditions. Simply put, he had made McGrath bowl where the Indians wanted him to, not where the bowler wanted to. Sachin took full toll of his loose deliveries and India got off to a runaway start in a game that they went on to win.

> On the field, you have to come up with innovative ideas because I am not used to getting into retaliation

and confrontation...I have engaged myself in these things when I have wanted to do so, not when the opposition wanted me to do so. There were a couple of occasions when I kept leaving the ball and I said that I was playing my game. It was strategy...The rest of the world thought that I was slow...I decide when I play the ball. The bowler does not decide that. Similarly, I decide when to speak to the bowler, not the bowler.

—Sachin Tendulkar, Hindustan Times Leadership Summit, December 2016

LEARNING TIP

Every chink in the opposition's armoury is there to be exploited for one's team. A leader sets the terms himself/herself, instead of functioning on those set by others.

Adjust and Adapt

Sachin was always mindful of the need to adjust and adapt to different personalities and situations. What holds true for sports, also holds true for non-sporting professions and life itself.

He led Mumbai Indians in the first four seasons of the Indian Premier League. The star-studded outfit did not live up to its reputation in the first two seasons in 2008 and 2009, failing to make it to even the semi-finals. The team management then decided to do something different on the eve of the 2010 season. As the captain, Sachin was the pivotal member of a 'bonding' workshop, which comprised interactive sessions in which the players reminisced about their early years in the game. The group also played different team sports, but not cricket.

The time spent in each other's company brought the players—senior and junior, Indian and overseas, legends and mortals—closer. They worked out what made each other tick, and how they could complement each other. The rapport that they established with each other in the lead-up to the tournament was reflected in their performances in the competition itself. Mumbai Indians had an outstanding season till the final, which they lost to Chennai Super Kings.

6

Reinvent to Remain Relevant

The Tendulkar Way

The daily drills, the emphasis on exercise, keeping one's eye on diet—doing all this for a quarter of a century is well-nigh unimaginable... If his cricketing shots were textbook, his behaviour can also be termed as a manual for good behaviour. In a world where icons, particularly sporting ones, are found to have feet of clay, this diminutive bloke has been unimpeachable in his conduct. He rarely gets angry, never loses his cool when he is being mobbed and always accepts the bouquets and brickbats with humility. I do not think we must restrict the exemplary nature of Tendulkar's behaviour to cricket or to India; it should be a lesson to sportsmen the world over.

—Sir Viv Richards, *The Week*,
1 December 2013

In the late 1990s, things were not looking very good for Amitabh Bachchan, the megastar of the Hindi film industry. His 'comeback' in 1997 after a self-imposed five-year exile, had not been a memorable one. His films were flopping and his film production and event management company was floundering. The debts were accumulating and his detractors were having a field day. Bachchan has gone on record to say how he was pondering over his options late in the night, when the solution suddenly presented itself.

He had essayed many a different and difficult role with aplomb in a distinguished acting career, but he had experienced setbacks in some 'roles' in real life. He had failed as an entrepreneur and undergone a forgettable stint in politics a decade before. It was time, he concluded, to return to 'being himself' and doing what he did best.

The following morning, Bachchan visited the residence of Yash Chopra, one of the most respected film-makers in the industry, with whom he had collaborated on several successful films in the 1970s and 1980s. The duo had not worked together for nearly two decades. The megastar asked the film-maker for a role. Chopra offered him the part of an obstinate patriarch in his next film, which was slated to release in the new millennium.

Another Indian legend was not having the best of times at around the same time. Sachin did not experience failure as acutely as Bachchan did, but he was far from happy in the latter stages of his first stint as captain of India. After beating South Africa at home in 1996–97, India were battered in the first two Tests of the 'return' series in the rainbow nation. Sachin did not allow the defeats to fluster him, and he continued to back his team. He was delighted when the Indian team outplayed the South Africans on the first four days of the third and final Test match at Johannesburg. The visitors were headed for victory on the final day, when the skies opened. Play resumed after a while, but the hosts managed to hang on. India were just 2 wickets short of victory when the umpires ruled that no further play was possible. Denied the opportunity to snatch a consolation win, India's twenty-three-year-old captain was devastated. He locked himself up in the washroom and broke down.

Greater shocks were in store for the skipper. Javagal Srinath, his premier strike bowler, was ruled out of the tour of the West Indies that followed, due to a shoulder injury. The paceman's absence notwithstanding, the Indians bowled well in the first two Tests and peaked in the third Test at Bridgetown, Barbados. All the Indian batsmen needed to do was score a mere 120 runs to register their first Test win in the Caribbean in twenty-one years. However, they were bowled out at 81. There was another insipid performance in an ODI at St. Vincent later on the tour. The Indians got off to a good start in pursuit of a target of 250 runs, only to surrender the game by losing their last eight wickets for 46 runs. The defeats at Bridgetown and St. Vincent cost India the Test and ODI series respectively.

The disappointed cricket-loving public in India was shocked when sections of the media dropped hints that some members of the team appeared to be rather indifferent to their disastrous performances. The captain, on the other hand, was putting too much pressure on himself by being far too harsh on himself. He appeared to be taking the setbacks personally.

It was probably the first time in Sachin's illustrious career that things were not happening the way he wanted them to. Of course, it wasn't that he had expected anything on a platter. However, it appeared that some elements in the team were not quite inclined to complement his efforts.

> I should be expecting from the players. If I am going to fight for the player then I have a right to expect from the player. I will try and support my players all the time but in return they too have to perform for me.
>
> —Sachin Tendulkar, *The Sportstar*, 3 May 1997

There was no let-up for him in the second half of 1997. In fact, things got progressively worse. He could not understand some of the bizarre calls taken by the national selectors and their penchant for contradicting themselves. A player who was dropped for being reckless on the West Indies tour was recalled two months later for a series in Sri Lanka, that too at the expense of a player who had batted well in a quadrangular tournament between the two tours.

It emerged in later years that one of the reasons the Indian team was so inconsistent during that phase was because some of its members had 'other priorities.' Not many take this fact into account when they go about branding Sachin as a 'great batsman but a poor captain.' Quite simply, a captain is only as good as his team. There was only so much that even an extraordinary cricketer like Sachin Tendulkar could have done; he could not have batted, bowled and fielded for those whose loyalties lay elsewhere.

All those who were convinced that Sachin would go from strength to strength as a captain after India's 4–1 victory over Pakistan in a limited-overs series in Canada in September 1997, were in for a disappointment. The national selectors sprung a surprise by 'instructing' him to bat in the middle order in a bilateral ODI series against Sri Lanka and a quadrangular tournament in Sharjah. Unfortunately for him, the team fared poorly.

> Sachin took some time to realize that it is not practical to expect others to emulate his feats. Basically, his talent was inborn and those skills cannot be acquired or transferred to anyone. The loss of any game under his captaincy worked him up so much that it preyed on his batting abilities.
>
> —Javagal Srinath, *India Today*, September 2010

DO WHAT YOU DO BEST...

The fact that Sachin scored over 1,000 runs in both forms of the game in the calendar year of 1997 did nothing to dispel the claims of his detractors that he had not been batting at his best while leading. On 2 January 1998, he underwent the mortification of learning from the media that he was no longer the captain. Any lesser mortal in his position could have sulked and brooded for days, but Sachin chose to handle the situation by reminding himself of who he was.

He tackled the situation by returning to his roots and making up his mind to concentrate on doing what he did best. While he had done all that he could to turn things around for his team as a captain, he had never been obsessed with that role. What he loved over and above everything else was batting; he was a batsman and a belligerent one at that, first and foremost.

Restored to the opening slot for a limited-overs tournament in Bangladesh, he essayed a succession of blazing innings, all of which rekindled memories of his best knocks at the top of the order, including the 82 runs off 49 balls against New Zealand at Auckland in March 1994.

Others may have perceived the loss of the captaincy as a setback, but Sachin viewed it as an opportunity.

LEARNING TIP

View a setback as an opportunity.

Things turn out best for the people who make the best of the way things turn out. Had Sachin continued to captain the side in early 1998, it might well have been difficult for him to prepare as elaborately as he did for the team's next assignment—a series against the mighty Australians.

He always aimed to solve the greater problem first. The smaller ones, he believed, would sort themselves out in the process. The greatest 'problem', as far as the Indians were concerned, was Shane Warne. Sachin was excited and inspired by the challenge of taking on the leggie, who was expected to be a handful on the spin-friendly Indian wickets. He forgot his frustrations of the recent past when he plunged himself headlong into the preparations for the series. The priority was to find a way to get the better of Warne and his wares.

The leg-spinner had come a long way since his Test debut at Sydney in January 1992, when Ravi Shastri and Sachin himself had treated him with disdain. Left out of the squad after two forgettable Tests against India, Warne had returned a few months later and cemented his place in the Australian team with match-winning performances against Sri Lanka and the West Indies. He had not looked back after bagging 34 wickets in the 1993 Ashes. He landed in India in early 1998 with 303 wickets in 64 Tests and the title of the 'Greatest Leg-Spinner of All Time' under his belt. However, there was unfinished business on his mind. There was only one Indian wicket—that of Ravi Shastri's—among the 303. He was eager, almost desperate to prove himself against the world's best players of spin, in their backyard.

Sachin decided to stay within the crease as much as he could and play the ball as late as possible. He decided to adopt an open, slightly two-eyed stance, outside the line of the leg-stump, to the leggie. Warne, Sachin knew, would seek to pitch the ball in the rough patch created by the footmarks of the bowlers operating from the other end. This patch, which was situated just outside the right-hander's leg-stump, also constituted a 'blind spot' for right-handed batsmen. An open stance, Sachin reasoned, would enable him to combat the 'drift' that Warne generated in the air, as well as the unpredictable bounce and turn he would extract after landing the ball in the rough patch.

Containing a bowler of Warne's calibre would not work; his attacking bowling could only be blunted by attacking batting. There was hardly any margin of error and therefore, it was critical that Sachin's timing and execution of strokes were spot-on. Sachin, therefore, requisitioned the help of local leg-spinners and left-arm spinners, all of whom spun the ball from the right-hander's leg-side to the off. Their brief was to land the ball in deliberately roughed-up patches in the practice nets. Sachin spent hours batting against them in the nets and honed horizontal-batting strokes like the pull, cut and slog-sweep.

He first played Warne in a three-day game between Mumbai and the visitors that preceded the first Test. He blasted a double century, his first in first-class cricket, and the leg-spinner conceded over a run-a-ball. Round one had gone in the Indian's favour, but Sachin noted that Warne did not land a single delivery in the rough patch created by the bowlers' footmarks. One legend was trying to outsmart another. There was no way Warne was going to reveal the ace that was up his sleeve in a three-day, 'side' game. Both were ready for each other when the first Test got underway at Chennai.

Sachin won his much-published bout with Warne, with scores of 4, 155*, 79, 177 and 31 in the Test series. The mission to neutralize the greatest leg-spinner in the history of the sport involved thorough planning and an incredible amount of hard work. This in turn ensured faultless execution. Sachin's subjugation of Warne was the highlight of 1998—one of the most successful years of his career.

LEARNING TIP

The key to success is meticulous planning, canny strategizing and an enormous amount of hard work.

Bouncing Back: Health Scares and Resurgence 2004–06

The period from 2004 to 2006 was a low phase for Sachin. He was diagnosed with a tennis elbow affliction in 2004 and he underwent a shoulder surgery in mid-2006. He was forced to miss quite a few matches as a result, and the hiatuses took their toll on his consistency with the bat. Staying away from

*Not out

a game he had loved all his life was an ordeal, and there were times when he feared the worst.

> I got operated on…and recovery took almost four to four-and-a-half months and in those months, a lot went through my mind. I thought I might not be able to hold a cricket bat again… I thought that this is the end of my career. I've had sleepless nights because of that, so I think that time was the toughest of my life to deal with and my family had a huge role to play there, especially my wife. She showed me the positive side of life where in 2004–05 I had already completed fifteen years and she told me that many guys don't last for fifteen months and here you've been able to play for fifteen years so you should be thankful to the Almighty for allowing you to play for fifteen years without [a] major injury and this is the first major injury you are dealing with. So not everything is lost, you will recover. That made a huge difference, it just changed the way I thought.
>
> —Sachin Tendulkar, *Bradman Museum and International Cricket Hall of Fame Interview*, 2010

His inconsistency during this phase delighted his critics. His fans were outraged when a prominent newspaper came up with a caption that went 'ENDULKAR' after India lost a Test to Pakistan at Karachi in early 2006. However, the man himself could not care less. He scored heavily in the ODI series that followed and was one of the chief architects of India's comprehensive 4–1 win over its traditional rival.

This was another instance of Sachin responding to a crisis of sorts by letting his bat do the talking for him. It was also another instance of him converting a setback into an opportunity. He utilized the time that he spent recuperating from his injuries and surgeries to think about the sport and what it meant to him. It was during this period that he steeled himself to get back to doing what he did best. He used the breaks that he was forced to take, to rediscover all the reasons that had made him fall in love with cricket, as a child. What he went on to achieve in the so-called 'twilight years' of his career was nothing short of sensational.

▪

A panel that comprised elite members of the international cricketing fraternity picked Sachin as the winner of the Sir Garfield Sobers Award for being the Cricketer of the Year, at the seventh annual ICC Awards Ceremony for 2009–10. He was thirty-seven years old then and had been playing international cricket for over two decades. He also received the People's Choice Award at the same function.

From January 2010 to January 2011, Sachin scored 1,722 runs from 15 Tests at an average of 82.00, inclusive of eight centuries of which two were doubles. In the same period, he also played four ODIs and scored a double century in one of them. In March 2012, a month before he turned thirty-nine, he became the first batsman to complete a century of international centuries.

What also sustained Sachin's passion for the sport for more than a quarter of a century was his quest for perfection. Sachin never lost sight of the fact that cricket, for all its emphasis on history and traditions, was a dynamic sport. Whether it was a club cricketer or an icon like Sachin Tendulkar, it is imperative to 'reinvent' oneself to ensure a long and fruitful innings in the game. The same holds true for every professional.

His propensity to do whatever he could to add newer facets to his game and repertoire was visible even at an early stage of his career. While staying with his uncle and aunt at their Shivaji Park home in the mid-1980s, he concocted an exercise to pass the time. He shaved a golf ball and got his aunt to hurl it at him. The ball would bounce sharply off the floor in different directions and Sachin would look to meet it with the full face of his bat. He had no option but to defend, given the presence of furniture and other items in the drawing room of the house. As the days passed, he realized that the drawing-room batting sessions with his aunt and the golf ball were helping him hone his back-foot defence. He mastered the art of defending with soft hands.

> I have not taken anything for granted. I have faced a number of challenges. It wasn't that it was a smooth path and I could just pick up a bat and go out and score runs and everything was fine. My family has been my strength right from my childhood—parents, siblings and then my wife and children. They have been rock-

solid. In difficult moments, they have been with me. There were many celebrations in my life, but nobody got carried away. Because they were balanced, I also figured out how to deal with success.

—BMW Presents Sachin Tendulkar,
March 2015

LEARNING TIP

Q: What was it that sustained Sachin's passion for the sport for more than a quarter of a century?

A: His quest for perfection.

Every professional should strive to do likewise.

Conquer Disappointment

Sachin encountered his first major disappointment in 1987, when he did not receive the Mumbai Cricket Association's annual award for the Best Junior Cricketer of the Year despite some extraordinary performances in the 1986–87 season. He even considered quitting the game in the heat of the moment and was assuaged by a letter of encouragement written by none other than Sunil Gavaskar, his childhood hero. What the 'boy wonder' achieved in the months to follow left him with neither the time nor the energy to recollect how disappointed he had been to miss out on the award. With his feats in the 1987–88 season, he ensured that not only those who had overlooked him for the award, but also the entire cricket-loving community in Mumbai and beyond, could not ignore him even if they wanted to.

The fourteen-year-old made the most of his apprenticeship as the 'baby' of Mumbai's Ranji Trophy squad in the same season. In the following weeks, he averaged a modest 1,025 from four games in the inter-school Harris Shield; the four-digit average was a consequence of his being dismissed only once in the four innings in which he achieved an aggregate of 1,025 runs, inclusive of two triple centuries. One of the triples was an unbeaten 326 that he scored in a stand of 664 with his schoolmate Vinod Kambli, which was the highest partnership in any class of cricket at the time. The boys became household names across the country and the rest, as they say, is history.

Penchant for preparation

'Training is everything,' said Mark Twain.

The man who plotted and executed the downfall of Shane Warne in the 1997–98 series between India and Australia would tailor his training as per the conditions he and his colleagues were likely to encounter in an upcoming series. Some of the training methods were unconventional, like the one he adopted on the eve of a tour of Australia, where he expected to encounter a quality pace attack on nippy wickets. A plastic sheet was spread on the 'batting' half of a wicket and doused with water. A group of bowlers, armed with rubber balls, was instructed to pitch every delivery short of a length. True to form, the rubber balls would take off after landing on the damp plastic sheet, and Sachin would duck, leave, cut and pull to his heart's content.

His penchant for preparation enabled Sachin to add new strokes to his repertoire. The highlight of his splendid innings of 155 against South Africa at Bloemfontein in 2001–02 was the way he used the steep bounce being generated by the opposition bowlers to his advantage. He simply guided the rising ball over the heads of the off-side cordon, to the boundary. Sachin essayed this 'uppercut' with aplomb for the remainder of his career. A few months later, he exhibited the 'switch hit' in an ODI against England, years before Kevin Pietersen was credited with 'inventing' it; the South Africa-born England batsman had only 'reinvented' it.

> When you become successful, you are simultaneously raising people's expectations, and you have to work the hardest to live up to those. My formula was that while I appreciate everything that has come my way, I need to find a way to push myself harder, continue to reinvent myself and continue the process of getting better, and if people have liked me for (having done) that, when what is the need to change?
>
> —BMW Presents Sachin Tendulkar,
> March 2015

Sachin epitomized invention and reinvention. This held true for Amitabh Bachchan as well. Shortly after he had started work on Yash Chopra's film, which was titled *Mohabbatein*, he received an offer to do something unprecedented. A leading media conglomerate had bagged the rights to produce the Indian version of *Who Wants to Be a Millionaire*, a quiz show for the common man that was very popular in the West. The conglomerate wanted the Indian edition to be hosted by someone who was a household name in the country and the 'Superstar of the Millennium' was the obvious choice. But then, the late 1990s was a time when television was looked down upon as a medium by the luminaries of the film industry. For many people, even the idea of Amitabh Bachchan appearing on the 'small screen' was anathema. However, the man in question decided to take a chance and with it, the opportunity. *Kaun Banega Crorepati* was a landmark in the history of Indian television. It has had nine seasons from 2000 to 2017, with Bachchan having hosted eight of those.

LEARNING TIP

It is critical to keep reinventing yourself as a professional.

Passing on the Mantle

Sachin's retirement as a cricketer in 2013 did not come in the way of his utilizing his experience and expertise to suggest ways in which the sport could reinvent itself and thereby enhance its chances of remaining relevant for future generations and facilitate the all-round development of its practitioners. This is a lesson all professionals—seasoned as well as aspiring—would do well to imbibe.

A few years ago, Sachin elicited extreme reactions when he suggested that all fourteen members of a cricket team be involved on the field in inter-school tournaments, instead of eleven playing and the other three sitting on the bench. He reckoned that the active participation of the entire team would ensure that every player would retain his/her enthusiasm for the sport, instead of having a situation where the reserve players could lose interest simply because they were doing nothing productive for days and weeks at a stretch. The Mumbai Schools Sports Association adopted the fourteen-player idea in inter-school tournaments in the 2016–17 season.

Another idea of his, which he believes could help Indian cricketers tide over the problem of adjustment that confronts them whenever they tour and play in alien conditions, is a lot more radical. He has suggested that the Kookaburra ball, which is used in countries like Australia, South Africa and New Zealand, be used in the first innings of domestic matches in India. This would give the batsmen and bowlers the opportunity to get acquainted with a type of ball that is different from the SG balls that they are used to playing with. That is not all. He recommends that the matches be played on different surfaces, with the first innings to be played on a hard, green and bouncy strip, and the second on a typically slow and low subcontinental wicket. The pacemen on either side would thus get to operate on a green-top with a Kookaburra, which is known to be a lot more effective than an SG on that type of wicket, in the first innings. On the other hand, the spinners in both camps would also pick up the tricks of bowling with a Kookaburra on a pace-friendly wicket. The SG ball, which has a more pronounced seam than its Kookaburra counterpart and is more conducive to spin bowling, will come into play in the second innings, where the action will shift from a green-top to a turning track. The fast bowlers will also reap the benefits of bowling with the SG ball, which 'reverse-swings' more effectively than the Kookaburra.

Sachin has also spoken at length about the need to reduce the imbalance between the bat and ball by producing more bowler-friendly pitches. There is reason to believe that the two-pitch and two-balls format that he has recommended, might help in this regard.

For instance, a captain who would otherwise be inclined to bowl first after winning the toss on a green-top, will have to bear in mind that if he does elect to bowl, then he and his players will have to bat last on a turning track.

LEARNING TIP

Professionals should share their knowledge and expertise with those who aspire to follow their footsteps. That is the least they can do to nurture the future of the vocation that has given them everything.

As of now, Sachin's 'two-pitch' and 'two-ball' idea has few takers. The majority seems to be of the view that first-class matches have a relevance of their own and ought not to be looked at as 'practice matches for international cricket'. However, it is unlikely that this will deter him from coming up with more ideas that he believes will benefit the sport in the long run.

Did cricket-lovers in the 1980s imagine that a time would come when a spinner would open the bowling in ODIs, or that twenty-overs-a-side matches would be played at the international level? However, these things are an integral part of the game today. Therefore, one does not know what will be introduced and eventually come to be accepted as conventional in the sport in the future. Life is all about change and reinvention, be it in cricket or any other field. A dynamic approach, like the one followed by Sachin throughout his career as a professional cricketer and beyond, is the stepping stone to success.

▪

Retired, but Not Done Yet

Sachin took oath as a member of the Rajya Sabha, the Upper House of India's Parliament in June 2012. He was the first active international sportsperson to be nominated for this honour. It was not that Sachin was unprepared for his 'second innings'. In fact, the idea of giving something back to society, especially its underprivileged sections, had been on his mind for a long time. In 2007, he was approached for an article on the 'India he dreamt of'. He articulated a seven-point agenda, which comprised the eradication of hunger, universal access to clean drinking water, the right to shelter, an end to discrimination against women and female infanticide, access to proper healthcare, the end of terror and a more tolerant India, accepting of its diversity.

Since 2014, Sachin has been involved in some fruitful ventures like the adoption of Puttamraju Kandrika, a village in Andhra Pradesh. He utilized the funds allotted to him to create infrastructure in the form of proper roads, storm water drains and even a playground. Measures were also taken to help some villagers resolve their addiction issues. He was part of *Spreading Happiness*, a project that sought to tap solar energy to provide electricity to far-flung areas. Thousands have benefited from the same already. Sachin has spoken on multiple fora about the need for Indians to discard their sedentary lifestyles and engage in physical and sporting activities. He has repeatedly emphasized that 'Swastha Bharat' (Fit India) is something that ought to go hand-in-hand with the 'Swachh Bharat' (Clean India) campaign initiated by the Union Government of India, of which he is an ambassador. The cricketing legend who spoke in monosyllables in his first TV interview in 1989 has metamorphosed into an accomplished orator, entrepreneur, mentor and an inspiration for professionals aspiring to excel in different fields. Today, Sachin is, for all practical purposes, a life-coach.

> The most important thing for me (after retirement) is that I am getting to do all the things that I couldn't do during my cricketing years. I am able to rub shoulders with all those people who were miles away from me. I am going to different parts of India as a Rajya Sabha MP. I visited the village that I adopted and understood what it is like to stay there. Life is completely different. It has been a learning experience... Overall, as a person, I think it has given me an opportunity to travel around and mingle with people and learn more things in life
>
> —Sachin Tendulkar,
> Hindustan Times Leadership Summit, 2016

Sachin has broadened his horizons and set new targets for himself after hanging up his cricketing boots. His 'first innings' was all about chasing his cricketing goals. He sees the end of a glorious chapter of his life as the 'beginning' of another that promises to be as—if not more—splendid.

LEARNING TIP

Life is all about change and reinvention,
be it in cricket or any other field.
A dynamic approach is the stepping stone to success.

7

Never Give Up

Being Perseverant, the Tendulkar Way

We had an excellent outfit in 2011 [World Cup]. We strategized, practised hard and most importantly, translated all that into performance on the field. Our performances kept getting better as the tournament progressed and peaked at precisely the right time. What we felt when the captain hit the winning six in the final was indescribable. I was touched when members of the team 'dedicated' the win to me. These are moments I will never ever forget.

—Sachin Tendulkar, *World Champions*,
BCCI, 2011

They say that it is easier to reach the top than to stay there. Individuals who come to be acknowledged as the best in their respective professions are invariably those who are resilient. They stare adversity in the eye and make it blink. The bigger the setback, the grander is their recovery. The bigger the stage and greater the pressure, the better they perform.

Sachin belonged to the generation that was inspired to take to cricket because of the seminal event that occurred on 25 June 1983. He was ten years old when 'Kapil's Devils' stunned the cricketing world by beating the West Indies in the final of the 1983 World Cup. The Indian team returned home to a rapturous welcome and the players were hailed as national heroes.

Sachin's association with cricket's premier quadrennial event witnessed many a masterclass in leadership, crisis management and also the one attribute that distinguishes the leaders from the followers—resilience.

He is only the second player after Javed Miandad of Pakistan to play in as many as six World Cups. The 1983 triumph was always at the back of his mind and he aspired to emulate his childhood heroes. It took him a while—a small matter of six World Cups and nearly a quarter of a century to fulfil his ambition. Yet, he never gave up. From 17 October 1987, the day he first watched a World Cup game 'in the flesh' as a ball-boy when India played Zimbabwe at the Wankhede Stadium in Mumbai, till 2 April 2011, when he realized his goal at the same venue in what was his last

World Cup game, he never gave up on his dream, on his team and on himself.

All the qualities that made Sachin Tendulkar the quintessential professional—which have been described in the preceding chapters of this book—were on show in his World Cup appearances.

His first 'hurrah' in the World Cup was an undefeated knock of 54 against Pakistan at Sydney in the 1992 edition, which was co-hosted by Australia and New Zealand. Batting first, India started well with fluent knocks by Ajay Jadeja and skipper Mohammed Azharuddin, but they stuttered in the middle overs of the innings. Sachin and Kapil Dev then came together to stitch a stand that enabled India to finish at a competitive 216–7. Pakistan lost 2 early wickets before Aamir Sohail and Javed Miandad came together for a partnership. The duo batted well to take their side past triple figures. Pakistan clearly held the upper hand at that stage and India needed a breakthrough. Sachin, their fifth bowler, gave them one by having Sohail caught at mid-wicket. That dismissal proved to be the turning point of the game, as Pakistan collapsed in the face of outstanding bowling and fielding and were bowled out for 173. Sachin was the undisputed 'Player of the Match' for his brilliant batting, tight bowling, propensity to assume leadership when it mattered, and for not giving up. With the bat, he and Kapil Dev resurrected the Indian innings after Vinod Kambli and Sanjay Manjrekar fell in the same over. With the ball, he made Sohail and Miandad work hard for every run, and eventually dismissed the former.

There was one unforgettable moment when he and Kapil Dev were batting together in the final overs of India's innings. The veteran all-rounder struck a boundary and as he retraced his steps to return to the batting crease, his partner patted him on the back. It was quite a sight to see an eighteen-year-old, who was in his third year of international cricket, do this to a thirty-two-year-old legend in his thirteenth year of international cricket! But then, what matters more than your age at the international level is how you perform as part of a team. Both Sachin and Kapil Dev were doing their best to take their team to a defendable score and were accordingly appreciating each other. Out in the middle, as members of the Indian cricket team, they were equals. In sports, age does not matter once you cross the boundary line; only your ability to do your designated job and deliver for your team on a consistent basis, does. The same holds true for every professional. Consistency and results matter; nothing else does.

LEARNING TIP

It does not matter how old you are.
What matters most is how you perform at the highest level as the member of a unit.

India won their next game of the competition as well, against Zimbabwe at Hamilton. Sachin bagged the Player of the Match Award for the second game in succession, for his innings of 81. However, his team's campaign went off the rails thereafter and India crashed out with only two wins under their belt. Pakistan, one of the teams India had beaten, went on to lift the trophy. Sachin's innings of 84 in the league encounter against New Zealand went in vain.

Keep Trying, Even When Others Fail

He was at his best in the next edition of the quadrennial event—the Wills World Cup 1996, which was held in India, Pakistan and Sri Lanka. By the time England took on New Zealand at Ahmedabad in the first game of the tournament on 14 February 1996, Sachin was firmly ensconced as India's limited-overs opener and all-format talisman. He lived up to his reputation and scored a record 523 runs in the competition. His 90 against Australia at Mumbai overshadowed his hundreds against Kenya and Sri Lanka. Chasing 254 against Australia, India started disastrously, with Damien Fleming dismissing Ajay Jadeja and Vinod Kambli with only 6 runs on the board. One more wicket at that stage, and it would have been very difficult for India to get back into the game.

India were 17–2 at the end of the eighth over. The required rate was climbing and something had to give. Their most valuable player responded to the crisis by doing what he did best.

Sachin turned the game on its head and brought the capacity crowd to its feet with an extraordinary counterattack. Bowlers were known to target a team's captain or premier batsman, the thinking being that the body will fold up if the head is severed. Something similar happened at the Wankhede Stadium on the evening of 27 February 1996. However, the perpetrator in this case was a batsman, and the person at the receiving end was the bowler. Sachin's prime target was not Damien Fleming, who had taken those early wickets, but Glenn McGrath, Australia's premier bowler, who had started his spell with three maiden overs.

Sachin took the spectators, McGrath included, by surprise, with what he did to the first ball of the ninth over of the innings. The delivery wasn't short enough to merit a pull, but Sachin utilized his reflexes to move across the crease and back, thereby 'converting' a delivery that had been pitched on a length, into one that was short. He pulled it over mid-on for four. Mark Taylor, the Australian captain, then stationed himself at short mid-wicket, where he had caught Sachin on earlier occasions. However, the batsman had learnt from his previous errors. He essayed another pull, ensuring that the ball was not within catching distance of the fielder as it flew past him. It was a stroke of genius in more ways than one; the coaching manuals advised that the pull be played off the back foot, but Sachin had essayed this one off the front foot. The ball thudded into the hoardings beyond the mid-wicket rope, even before anybody had the time to react. McGrath, flustered after the two strokes, then served a rare full-toss which was duly driven past cover for four. This was proof of the fact that Sachin was succeeding in his endeavour to make the bowler bowl where he wanted him to. McGrath, who had not conceded a run in his first 3 overs, went for 27 runs in his fifth and sixth overs. The assault was a precursor of sorts to what Sachin did against Shane Warne when the Australians returned to India for a full series in early 1998.

The offensive forced Taylor to introduce Shane Warne, his trump-card, into the attack, a little earlier than he had wished, but the change made no difference. India's talisman cantered to 90 runs off 84 balls before he was stumped. India's defeat in the game, as in the two encounters against Sri Lanka in which Sachin scored 137 and 65 respectively, reflected poorly on the team and its inability to complement its mainstay.

India made it to the semi-finals in 1996 World Cup, but they fell well short of getting into the final four in the next edition of the tournament in 1999.

▪

Nation Before Self

The seventh edition of the World Cup was played in the United Kingdom in 1999. The Indian team was scheduled to play Zimbabwe at Leicester after losing its first game to South Africa at Brighton. Hours before the game, news came through of the demise of Professor Ramesh Tendulkar, the man who had shaped the history of the sport by letting his son 'be himself'.

Sachin, devastated by the tragedy, flew home and missed the Zimbabwe game, which his team lost. With two defeats from two games, India's only hope of qualifying for the Super Sixes—the next stage of the competition—was to beat Kenya, Sri Lanka and England comprehensively in their remaining league games.

The Indian team management and the BCCI had decided not to disturb Sachin in his hour of grief. It was Sachin's mother who convinced him to fly back to England. For him, the clincher was a reminder that even his father, whom he would never see again, would have liked him to return to England to try and put his team's campaign back on track. Millions of cricket-lovers had goose pimples when it was announced that Sachin had put his team and country ahead of self and was joining the team. Leaving his bereaved family behind would have been tough, but he did not allow that to come in the way of doing his duty. He was by no means the only individual to have tears in his eyes when he completed a century against Kenya at Bristol. It was a stirring illustration of a professional responding to his duty towards nation (and profession) with grit, gumption and grace, despite encountering a personal crisis.

LEARNING TIP

A professional responds to calls of duty with grit, gumption and grace, regardless of what he/she may be going through on the personal front.

Team India came within one step of scaling the summit in the next edition of the quadrennial event. The best performer of the ICC Cricket World Cup 2003, which was co-hosted by South Africa, Zimbabwe and Kenya, was Sachin, who amassed 673 runs, exactly 150 more than his 1996 tally.

He had batted in the middle order in the months leading up to the event because his team had requested him to. Egged on by Javagal Srinath and Anil Kumble, John Wright, India's coach, sought Sachin out before the start of the tournament and asked him where he would like to bat. Sachin's response was that he would bat wherever the team wanted him to. When Wright persisted, Sachin reluctantly admitted that 'if he were given the choice', then he would like to open.

Would he have batted as outstandingly in the competition had he not been restored to the opening slot? Yes, most certainly! For him, the team always came before self.

> During the 2003 World Cup, I went to his room at Sandton Hotel at Johannesburg. It was a huge room with a big double bed, but Tendulkar was sleeping on the floor carpet with a thin pillow and a towel, because he was suffering from a backache. He was so eager to win the World Cup that he decided to make a few sacrifices along the way.
>
> —Debasish Datta, *Outlook Special Commemorative Issue*, 2010

Braving Ills, Braving Illness

Apart from the issues with his back, Sachin also had problems with his ankle, which he had injured on the tour of New Zealand, a couple of months previously. Strapping the ankle before every practice session and match was an ordeal, and the wound would sting when it would come in contact with seawater during the team's recovery sessions on the beach. He had a torn ligament and tendon in a finger, which made it difficult for him to even hold a cup of tea properly. He also had a strained hamstring, due to which he could not jog or sprint with his teammates and had to cycle instead. But then, he viewed all these as minor irritants. These were not going to affect him and his resolve to go the distance.

The Indian team did not get off to the best of starts in the tournament. A lacklustre victory over Holland was followed by a shoddy performance against Australia. The defending champions bowled India out for 125 and won by 9 wickets. Sourav Ganguly and his men still had four more league matches left to make a bid for qualifying to the 'Super Sixes' stage of the tournament, but their detractors were determined to make a splash after the fiasco against Australia. What ensued was as horrendous as it was ridiculous. Effigies of the players were burnt and houses of some stoned. Some former players also joined the bandwagon, slamming the Indian players as if they had committed an act of terrorism. Members of the Indian media were also not endearing themselves to the players with the questions that they were posing at media conferences.

Sachin was neither the captain nor the vice-captain, but in terms of stature, he had no equal in the squad. Being someone who valued a leader's responsibilities more than his entitlements, there was no question of his not standing up for his teammates when the situation demanded the same.

Members of the fourth estate were surprised when he strode into the media conference hall before his team's next game of the tournament, against Zimbabwe at Harare. He proceeded to read out the following message:

> We ourselves are disappointed with the kind of performance we all have put up. I also understand the disappointment you have gone through. I am just here to assure you that we will be fighting till the last ball is bowled.

Having made a statement, literally and figuratively, he exited the hall. John Wright, the then coach of the Indian team, likened the statement to a 'papal pronouncement' in his memoirs. There was no other member of the Indian team who could have silenced the rabble-rousers and boosted the spirits of the supporters, the way Sachin did by uttering those three sentences.

LEARNING TIP

The best of leaders reserve their best for a crisis.

Having made a statement off the field, Sachin and his teammates set out to do likewise on it. He scored a match-winning 81 against Zimbabwe and starred in India's next two games as well, with knocks of 152 against Namibia and 50 against England. His teammates put up a splendid show with the bat, ball and in the field, and they sealed a spot in the 'Super Sixes' with four wins from five games. However, they were aware that a reverse in their next game could push them back to square one, not in the points table, but certainly mentally. On the other hand, a victory in what was for all practical purposes, a final before the final, would give them a shot in the arm on the eve of the second stage of the tournament.

Streets across the subcontinent wore a deserted look on the afternoon of 1 March 2003, when Sourav Ganguly accompanied Waqar Younis, his Pakistani counterpart, for the toss at the SuperSport Park, Centurion. Waqar won the toss and opted to bat, and Pakistan scored 273–7. History was not on India's side. Their previous highest successful chase in the World Cup was 222.

Sachin shut himself off from the world in the break. He padded up, plugged on his earphones and told the 12th man to alert him when it was time to leave the dressing-room. As they made their way to the middle, Sachin reminded Virender Sehwag, his opening partner, that they needed to be cautious in the initial overs. Sehwag agreed with his senior's assessment that the Pakistanis would go flat out for wickets in the opening overs.

Sachin usually did not take strike when he opened in ODIs, but the significance of the occasion prompted him to do something different to try and seize the initiative. He decided to face Wasim Akram's first ball. To those watching, it was a stirring display of leadership, even before he had faced a ball.

He struck a boundary in the very first over and then took a single. When he crossed over to the non-striker's end, the umpire asked him why he had taken strike. Sachin's reply said it all: 'I want to impose myself on this match.' The leader had made a statement. Sehwag also hit a boundary in Akram's first over.

In the second over, Sachin faced Shoaib Akhtar, the fastest bowler in the world. After three uneventful balls, Sachin struck him for a six over third-man. He followed it with a flick for four and then a defensive push, which was timed so well that he got another boundary. Shoaib, clearly shell-shocked by Sachin's assault, was taken off after just one over and Waqar brought himself on from his end. Sehwag struck the Pakistani captain's first delivery over the covers for six.

The Indian openers had realized by then that the bowling was not up to the mark. Therefore, it made sense to abandon plan A and implement plan B instead. Their ability to alter their game plan enabled them to take the game away from their opponents in next to no time. The horse had bolted by the time the Pakistanis came to terms with what had happened. India did not lose the psychological advantage even when Waqar dismissed Sehwag and Ganguly fell in quick succession. The pressure of playing the 'arch enemy' had brought out the best in Sachin, who kept sending the spectators, TV viewers and commentators into raptures with his strokes.

He batted fluently until his hamstring started acting up. The obvious thing to do was to ask for a runner, but then, he had always been reluctant to ask for one, his reasoning being that his mind was his own and there was no way a runner would know what was going on in it.

Sachin's dedication to his craft boosted his anticipatory skills to incredible levels. India were touring England in 2007 when the TV broadcaster acted on a hunch and maxed the volume of the stump microphones when he was on strike. The crew was stunned to hear him utter the exact number of runs he expected to score from a delivery even before he made contact with the ball! It appeared that Sachin knew what he would do with the ball as soon as it was released by the bowler. He could not have reached this level of batting perfection merely on the strength of his talent. He had worked hard to get there.

Against Pakistan at Centurion in the 2003 World Cup, Sachin eventually asked for a runner, but he fell soon after for 98. His teammates completed what he had started and took India to victory with plenty of overs to spare.

India played brilliantly in the subsequent games and took on Australia, the only team they had lost to in the competition, in the final at Johannesburg. India won the toss and elected to field, but the decision backfired as the

Australians batted magnificently to amass 359–2. Sachin fell in the very first over of India's innings and it was an uphill struggle thereafter. He made no secret of the fact that he would have traded his 673 runs in the tournament and the Player of the Tournament Award for the World Cup.

Never Give Up Dreaming

The ICC Cricket World Cup 2007, played in the West Indies, was a disaster for India. Sachin was disappointed enough after his team's first-round exit in the tournament to consider retirement, but Ajit, his elder brother, reminded him that he had a few more peaks left to conquer. The 2011 edition of the World Cup was to be played on home turf. The prospect of making it to the final, which was to be played in Mumbai, his hometown, and winning the game, fired Sachin's imagination. With the benefit of hindsight, it will not be inappropriate to state that he started thinking about the 2011 World Cup, in 2007 itself. He was of course mindful of the fact that he was in his mid-30s and therefore had to work even harder on his fitness and consistency. He had of course, never taken his place in the team for granted. His performances in Tests and ODIs from May 2007 to January 2011 were nothing short of outstanding.

It is said of Prakash Padukone, India's Badminton legend, that he and his coaches 'planned his entire life' around winning the All-England Open, Badminton's Holy Grail. Their perseverance bore fruit when Padukone won the title in 1980. Sachin probably did something similar in the period from 2007 to 2011.

Centuries against England and South Africa at the league stage were followed by an 85 against Pakistan in the semi-final of the 2011 World Cup. He provided the team with many a sound start, especially in the quarter-final and final against Australia and Sri Lanka respectively.

He also contributed to the triumph with something that he did off the field. With Irfan Pathan losing form and consistency and slipping off the radar at the turn of the decade, the Indian team divided the fifth bowler's responsibilities between his brother Yusuf Pathan and Yuvraj Singh. The left-handed Yuvraj, whose brand of left-arm spin had broken many a stubborn partnership in the past, was assigned the prominent role of the two.

It had not been the best of times for Yuvraj, on and off the field. He had been in and out of the limited-overs side in 2010, and the selectors had given up on him as a Test batsman long back. Three years after 'vice-captaining' the team that won the inaugural World Twenty20, he had been superseded by Gautam Gambhir. Off the field, things weren't great either. He was troubled by nausea and would throw up blood quite frequently. That he had continued to play despite his health issues spoke volumes about his character.

On the eve of the first game of the tournament, against Bangladesh at Dhaka, Yuvraj was invited for dinner by his hero. Sachin, who had been playing for India for more than a decade before Yuvraj made his international debut, gave his junior colleague a pep talk and impressed upon him the value that he could add to the side with his batting, bowling and fielding. Even the most successful of players needed someone they admired to motivate them, and Yuvraj was no exception.

Sachin's man-management was spot-on. Yuvraj delivered so brilliantly with the bat and ball that he was declared the Player of the Tournament. The enormity of what he achieved for his team and country in the 2011 World Cup came to light a year later, when a malignant tumour was detected between his lungs, necessitating rounds of chemotherapy. The left-hander had declared after a league game of the tournament that he wanted to win the World Cup for 'someone special'; he revealed after the final that the 'special' individual was none other than the team's talisman, Sachin Tendulkar.

Sachin's single-mindedness had been contagious. His colleagues in the Indian team, all of whom had grown up idolizing him, had willed themselves to win the title for their hero, talisman and leader.

Moments after Mahendra Singh Dhoni hit the winning runs in the final of the tournament, Virat Kohli, currently India's captain, spoke for pretty much the entire Indian team, when he said that it was time the boys carried Sachin, considering that he had carried the burden of the nation (expectations) for twenty-one years.

Kohli and his teammates proceeded to walk the talk. An entire stadium and international TV audience cheered as Sachin did a lap of the Wankhede Stadium, perched on the shoulders of his teammates. It was a befitting tribute to an icon and an inspiration.

> Cricket taught me a lot of things... Cricket taught me to prepare for an event, to plan how I want to move forward and then, to be able to execute those plans was even more important. It taught me to respect your opposition and teammates.
>
> —Sachin Tendulkar at the 50th Inter IIT Sports Meet in 2014

LEARNING TIP

Never give up.

Annexures

SACHIN TENDULKAR FACTFILE
(Compiled by Sudhir Vaidya and Devendra Prabhudesai)

Full name: Sachin Ramesh Tendulkar
Born: 24 April 1973, Mumbai, Maharashtra
Prominent teams: India, Mumbai, West Zone, Rest of India, Yorkshire, Mumbai Indians
Nicknames/Appellations: Tendlya, Little Champion, God of Cricket, Sachu, Master
Batting style: Right-hand batsman
Bowling style: Right-arm off-break, Leg-break googly, Medium pace

Prominent Awards and Distinctions

1. Bharat Ratna: India's highest civilian honour, 2014.
2. Padma Vibhushan: India's second-highest civilian honour, 2008.

3. Padma Shri: India's fourth-highest civilian honour, 1998.
4. Rajiv Gandhi Khel Ratna Award in Sports and Games (India's highest sporting honour), 1998.
5. Honorary Group Captain: Indian Air Force, 2010 (the first individual from a non-aviation background to be accorded this distinction).
6. Arjuna Award for Sporting Excellence by the Government of India, 1994.
7. The ICC's Sir Garfield Sobers Award for being the International Player of the Year, 2009–10.
8. The BCCI's Polly Umrigar Award for being the Indian Cricketer of the Year in 2006–07 and 2009–10.
9. Maharashtra Bhushan: The highest civilian award given by the Government of the State of Maharashtra, 2001.
10. Membership of the Order of Australia, 2012.
11. Listed among the '100 Most Influential People in the World' by *TIME* magazine in May 2010.

Sachin Tendulkar in International Cricket

Batting and Fielding

	Matches	Inns	NO	Runs	HS	Avg	100s	50s	Cts
Tests	200	329	33	15,921	248*	53.78	51	68	115
ODIs	463	452	41	18,426	200*	44.83	49	96	140
T20Is	1	1	0	10	10	10.00	0	0	1

Notes

Inns: Innings

*: Not out

HS: Highest score

Cts: Catches held

Bowling

	Matches	Inns	Balls	Runs	Wkts	BBI	BBM	Avg	4w	5w
Tests	200	145	4,240	2,492	46	3/10	3/14	54.17	0	0
ODIs	463	270	8,054	6,850	154	5/32	5/32	44.48	4	2
T20Is	1	1	15	12	1	1/12	1/12	12.00	0	0

Notes

BBI: Best bowling figures in an innings
BBM: Best bowling figures in a match
4W: Four wickets in an innings
5W: Five wickets in an innings

Sachin Tendulkar in First-Class Cricket

Sunil Gavaskar scored 25,785 runs from 349 first-class matches, the highest by an Indian. Sachin Tendulkar is a close second, with 25,239 runs from 304 first-class matches.

Batting and Fielding

Matches	Inns	NO	Runs	HS	Avg	100s	50s	Cts
304	483	51	25,239	248*	58.42	81	116	173

Notes

NO: Not out
HS: Highest score
Cts: Catches held

Bowling

Balls	Runs	Wkts	BBI	Avg	4w	5w
7,561	4,357	70	3/10	62.24	0	0

Notes:
BBI: Best bowling figures in an innings
4W: Four wickets in an innings
5W: Five wickets in an innings

Sachin Tendulkar Trivia

- He is the only batsman to score a century on debut in India's three domestic first-class competitions—the Ranji Trophy, Duleep Trophy and Irani Cup.
- He was India's 187th Test cricketer and the youngest. He was only sixteen years and 205 days old when he made his Test debut.
- He is the youngest Indian to score a Test century. He was seventeen years and 112 days old when he scored an unbeaten 119 against England at Manchester in 1990.
- He is the first cricketer to complete a double century of Test appearances.
- He is the only batsman to score 100 international centuries (51 in Tests and 49 in ODIs).
- He was the first cricketer to complete the treble of 10,000 runs, 100 wickets and 100 catches in ODIs.
- He was the first batsman to score 12,000, 13,000, 14,000 and 15,000 runs in Tests.
- He was the first batsman to score 10,000, 11,000, 12,000, 13,000, 14,000, 15,000, 16,000, 17,000 and 18,000 runs in ODIs.
- He is only the fifth Indian, after Maharshi Dhondo Keshav Karve (1958), Dr Visvesvaraya (1960), Mother Teresa (1980) and Rajiv Gandhi (centenary of the Indian

National Congress, 1985) to feature on a postage stamp during his lifetime.

- Four years after his retirement, the Board of Control for Cricket in India (BCCI) paid him a unique tribute by retiring the No. 10 jersey, which he was synonymous with.
- Among the popular brands endorsed by him are Boost, Pepsi, Adidas, Coke, MRF, Britannia, Luminous Power Technologies, Musafir.com, BMW and Aviva Life Insurance.

Bibliography

Books

Prabhudesai, Devendra. 2017. *Hero: A Biography of Sachin Ramesh Tendulkar.* New Delhi: Rupa Publications.

Wright, John; Ugra, Sharda; Thomas, Paul. 2006. *John Wright's Indian Summers*. New Delhi: Penguin Books.

Mumbai's 500th Ranji Trophy Match, MCA, 2017.

Chappell, Greg. 2011. *Fierce Focus*. Australia: Hardie Grant Books.

World Champions, BCCI, 2011.

Tendulkar, Ajit. 1996. *The Making of a Cricketer—Formative Years of Sachin Tendulkar in Cricket*. Mumbai: Sachin Tendulkar Promotions Pvt Ltd.

Tendulkar, Sachin. 2014. *Sachin Tendulkar: Playing It My Way*. London: Hodder & Staughton.

Newspapers and Periodicals

India Today
Open
Outlook
Sportsweek
Sportsworld
The Hindu
The Indian Express
The Sportstar
The Times of India
The Week
Wisden Asia Cricket
Wisden Cricket Monthly

Websites

www.cricinfo.com
www.youtube.com
www.radhanathswami.net
www.smh.com.au
www.wikipedia.com

Films

Sachin: A Billion Dreams (Ravi Bhagchandka and Carnival Motion Pictures under 200 NotOut Productions, 2017)